PRACTICAL PET CARE HANDBOOK

SMALL PETS

PRACTICAL PET CARE HANDBOOK

SMALL PETS

david alderton

LORENZ BOOKS

This edition is published by Lorenz Books.

Lorenz Books is an imprint of Anness Publishing Ltd
Hermes House, 88–89 Blackfriars Road, London SE1 8HA
tel. 020 7401 2077; fax 020 7633 9499
www.lorenzbooks.com; info@anness.com

© Anness Publishing Ltd 2002, 2004

UK agent: The Manning Partnership Ltd,
6 The Old Dairy, Melcombe Road, Bath BA2 3LR;
tel. 01225 478444; fax 01225 478440; sales@manning-partnership.co.uk

UK distributor: Grantham Book Services Ltd,
Isaac Newton Way, Alma Park Industrial Estate,
Grantham, Lincs NG31 9SD;
tel. 01476 541080; fax 01476 541061; orders@gbs.tbs-ltd.co.uk

North American agent/distributor: National Book Network,
4501 Forbes Boulevard, Suite 200, Lanham, MD 20706;
tel. 301 459 3366; fax 301 429 5746; www.nbnbooks.com

Australian agent/distributor: Pan Macmillan Australia,
Level 18, St Martins Tower, 31 Market St, Sydney, NSW 2000;
tel. 1300 135 113; fax 1300 135 103;
customer.service@macmillan.com.au

New Zealand agent/distributor: David Bateman Ltd,
30 Tarndale Grove, Off Bush Road, Albany, Auckland;
tel. (09) 415 7664; fax (09) 415 8892

Publisher: Joanna Lorenz
Managing Editor: Judith Simons
Project Editor: Sarah Ainley
Photography: John Daniels
Designer: Michael Morey
Jacket Design: Balley Design Associates
Illustrator: Julian Baker
Index: Helen Snaith
Editorial Reader: Richard McGinlay
Production Controller: Claire Rae

Previously published as *Caring for Your Small Pets*

10 9 8 7 6 5 4 3 2 1

The author and publishers have made every effort to ensure
that all advice given in this book is accurate and safe, but
they cannot accept liability for any injury, damage or loss to
persons or property resulting from the keeping of any
of the featured pets.

CONTENTS

INTRODUCTION

The vast majority of small mammals that are popular as pets belong to the rodent family. The word "rodent" comes from the Latin word *rodere*, meaning "to gnaw", and describes the very sharp pair of chisel-shaped incisor teeth found in each jaw right at the front of the mouth. The shape and strength of these teeth is crucial to the survival of rodents as they enable them to crack seeds and nuts easily. Unlike our teeth, they continue growing throughout the rodent's life. This is essential to stop them from wearing down, which would prevent the rodent from eating.

Rabbits are not actually rodents, but are grouped instead with hares and pikas in a separate family known as lagomorphs. However, the structure of their teeth is very similar to that of rodents, except that they have a further tiny set of incisors each side of the main teeth at the front of the mouth.

Most rodents are relatively small in size, which makes them vulnerable to larger predators. As a result, they have keen senses to help them avoid detection. Their hearing is very acute, and they often communicate with each other using ultrasonic calls, which we are unable to hear because the frequencies are too high for our ears. They also have a very keen sense of smell. However, rodents generally have poor vision, since they spend much of their time hidden away in burrows during the day, emerging to forage for food at night.

◆ OPPOSITE
Guinea pigs are friendly rodents and they make excellent pets. They are suitable for housing either in outdoor accommodation or indoors in the home.

◆ LEFT
Rabbits come in a wide variety of sizes and colours. They are easy to care for, and an increasing number of owners are now keeping rabbits as indoor companions.

RABBITS

The rabbit is the most popular of all the small mammals kept as pets, thanks in part to its friendly nature. An ever-increasing range of breeds and colour varieties, many of which are likely to be on view at shows, has served to enhance their appeal both to breeders and pet-seekers. Rabbits have also proved to be very adaptable pets, with individuals settling well either in an outdoor hutch or as house-rabbits in the home.

INTRODUCTION

There are 25 different species of wild rabbit found around the world, but the ancestor of all today's domestic breeds is the Old World rabbit (*Oryctolagus cuniculus*), which was originally found in the Mediterranean region. At first, rabbits were kept as a source of food, in large outdoor enclosures. It is unclear when they were first brought to northern Europe; they may have been originally introduced by the invading Roman armies, but there is no evidence of an established wild population until after 1066.

Rabbits were originally valued for their fur and as a source of meat, and it was not until the late 1800s that they became popular with breeders as pets. By this stage, a number of the distinctive varieties were already established and, as a legacy from this era, the breeds today are often classified on the basis of fur or fancy, with the former group featuring those

which were originally kept for food. The advent of the killer viral disease myxomatosis in the 1950s altered the public's attitude to rabbit meat,

however, as the sight of sick and dying rabbits in the wild was very distressing.

As a result of changing perceptions, the rabbit has evolved into the most popular of all small animal pets, due to its friendly nature and attractive appearance. There are now more than 200 breeds in existence, some of which are very rare, while others are still being developed. One of the latest to be added to this list is the lionhead, a relatively small rabbit with a lion-like mane on its head. Unfortunately, some breeds have also become extinct, such as the angevin, which was the largest breed of rabbit ever known. Individuals were said to have a leg span of nearly 1.2 m (4 ft), and could weigh as much as 15 kg (33 lb).

Most breeds are short-coated, although the angora, which has been kept for centuries for its wool, is long-coated and needs special care to prevent its coat from becoming matted. Any rabbit that has an angora breed in its ancestry, such as the cashmere lop, must be groomed on a daily basis. Most other rabbits, however, do not need much grooming.

RABBITS AS PETS

All breeds of rabbit make appealing pets, although it is not a good idea to buy an adult rabbit without knowing its age. Start out with a youngster that is approximately nine or ten weeks old. At this age, the rabbit is fully

♦ ABOVE AND LEFT
The European wild rabbit, from which all of today's domestic breeds and varieties have been created. Domestication of the rabbit began thousands of years ago.

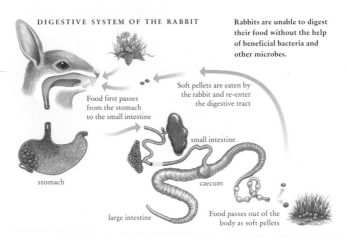

DIGESTIVE SYSTEM OF THE RABBIT

Rabbits are unable to digest their food without the help of beneficial bacteria and other microbes.

Food first passes from the stomach to the small intestine

Soft pellets are eaten by the rabbit and re-enter the digestive tract

small intestine

stomach

caecum

large intestine

Food passes out of the body as soft pellets

independent, but is still young enough to be tamed readily. Older rabbits that are not used to being handled are likely to be nervous and may never settle as pets. A rabbit will usually live for between six and eight years.

If, however, you are hoping to breed from your rabbit for show purposes, you will need to acquire older rabbits, although it may be better to start out with youngsters and wait for them to mature. It is generally better to start out with a doe (female) if you intend to breed rabbits for shows because, if necessary, you can arrange for her to be mated with

someone else's buck (male). However, most breeders are not keen to part with their best does.

Before buying any rabbit, always check its condition. The ears should be clean and clear of scabs, which can indicate an ear mite infestation. The eyes should be free from discharge, as should the nose. It is also important to part the lips so you can check the incisor teeth. If these are misaligned, you will have to have them trimmed back regularly throughout the rabbit's life. Check that the claws are not overgrown and that there are no sore patches on the underside of the hind legs. It is important to make sure that there is no sign of staining on the fur surrounding the vent, as this can indicate a digestive upset, which can be serious.

◆ ABOVE LEFT
Rabbits in the wild are very alert, since they face many dangers. The position of their eyes helps them to see well, while their tall ears detect and pinpoint the source of sounds accurately.

◆ BELOW
It is vital to consider size when choosing a rabbit. The larger breeds, such as the British giant, shown here with a Netherland dwarf, may be too big for younger children to handle easily.

◆ ABOVE
The sharp incisor teeth allow the rabbit to nibble plant matter, which is then ground up by molar teeth further back in the mouth.

9

A SELECTION OF SMALLER BREEDS

Rabbits today vary in size from the Flemish giant, which can tip the scales at 10 kg (22 lb), down to the tiny Netherland dwarf, which typically weighs about 900 g (2 lb). It is not just a matter of size, however, because breeds do differ significantly in temperament, and it is important to bear this in mind, especially if you are choosing a pet for a child. While the bigger breeds are generally placid, their size can make them difficult for a child to handle safely, and since rabbits are very susceptible to injury through falls, it is a better idea to choose a smaller breed for younger owners.

THE DUTCH

Although not as small as today's dwarf breeds, the Dutch, which weighs up to 2.5 kg (5½ lb), has long been a popular choice with rabbit enthusiasts. While pet owners enjoy its friendly nature, exhibitors are challenged by its highly distinctive coat markings.

The Dutch has a broad white area of fur encircling the front of the body, a half-coloured rear and white feet. The head and ears are coloured, with a distinctive white blaze extending down over the nose to the jaws. Dutch rabbits are currently bred in eight

colours. The dark shades, such as black or blue, are generally preferred to lighter shades, such as yellow. Rabbits with good fur markings can be identified while still hairless newborns, as the white areas can be recognized by their lighter pink skin coloration.

THE ENGLISH

The ever-popular English is the oldest of the fancy breeds, dating back as far as the early 1800s. It has a dark stripe running down its back to the base of the tail, with a variable pattern of spots on its sides, particularly on the hindquarters. There are several varieties, including black, blue and chocolate, plus a tortoiseshell. The ears are dark, as is the muzzle, with an area of dark fur usually encircling the eyes. The English is friendly, and the does usually make good mothers.

THE NETHERLAND DWARF

The breed known as the Netherland dwarf, which evolved from the Polish breed during the late 1800s, did not

THE REX

The smooth, soft, sleek coat of the rex rabbit meant that it was originally very popular with furriers, but today, the rex has become a common sight at rabbit shows, and is now bred in a large range of colours and markings. The mini rex is a smaller version of the rex itself and, at only half its weight, tips the scales at up to 1.8 kg (4 lb). The rex's thin coat means that it needs snug winter quarters in temperate climates. Make sure that these rabbits have sufficient bedding on the floor of their hutch; the fur below the hocks on the hind legs may otherwise become thin, and this can be the cause of recurring soreness, which can prove troublesome to both you and your rabbit over the course of its lifetime.

◆ LEFT
When deciding to buy a Netherland dwarf, inspect the teeth very carefully; these rabbits are vulnerable to malocclusion, and this will be a lifelong problem.

◆ BELOW
A fawn dwarf lop. Unlike some of the bigger lops, its ears are relatively short. The breed's friendly nature has made it very popular.

◆ BOTTOM
The fur of rex rabbits is short with a velvety feel as these rabbits lack the longer, coarse guard hairs seen in other breeds.

become well known until the 1950s. In some parts of Europe it is known as the dwarf Polish.

The Netherland dwarf is the smallest of today's breeds. Now available in a huge range of colours, this breed has a characteristic compact nose and short ears. The breed is perhaps not always as friendly as others of a similar size.

DWARF LOP

This breed has grown in popularity over recent years, thanks to its gentle disposition. The appeal of the dwarf lop has been enhanced by its floppy ears, which hang down the sides of its head but do not touch the ground. The dwarf lop is a scaled-down version of the larger French lop, and was created during the 1950s in the Netherlands. Young dwarf lops are born with upright ears that start to trail down as they grow older. In turn, they have been bred to create the even smaller mini lop, which was first recognized for show purposes in 1994.

A SELECTION OF LARGER BREEDS

With the growing interest in keeping rabbits in the home, larger breeds have become very popular, and they can be given plenty of space to roam. Some of these rabbits are larger and heavier in size that a small dog. As an example, the British giant, closely-related to the Flemish giant, weighs up to 6.1 kg (15 lb). The breed originated from stock kept as long ago as the 1500s around the city of Ghent in Belgium.

FLEMISH GIANT

The traditional colour of the Flemish giant is steel grey, and it was the refusal of the British show authorities

to recognize this breed in other colours that originally triggered the development of the British giant strain in the 1930s. The Flemish giant is still better known internationally, and is also slightly heavier, averaging 7–8 kg (15½–17½ lb). These large rabbits are known to be friendly, with calm temperaments. As house-rabbits they will settle quickly into a domestic lifestyle, and can be trained to use a litter tray from an early age. Although the typical agouti-patterned form, resembling that of the wild rabbit, is commonly seen, a range of colours from pure white through to blue and black is available as well.

✦ ABOVE
Large breeds of rabbit like this British giant are back in fashion, thanks to growing interest in keeping house-rabbits. The British giant is ideal for this purpose, but can be rather large for a small child to handle.

✦ LEFT
A white New Zealand rabbit. This breed is characterized partly by its relatively coarse, shaggy coat as well as its pink eyes. These rabbits have a steady temperament and make good pets.

NEW ZEALAND VARIETIES

Several varieties of rabbit have their origins in New Zealand. The original white variety was created as a meat breed. It has a well-muscled body and relatively short ears, typically weighing up to 5.4 kg (12 lb). These rabbits grow very quickly and are capable of reaching almost half their adult weight by just ten weeks of age. They are

◆ BELOW
The similarity to a true hare can be seen in this Belgian hare, although it is a pure rabbit breed. These rabbits became immensely popular in the United States in the early 20th century.

an attractive silky texture, with individual hairs that are over 2.5 cm (1 in) long. The traditional colour is a pale shade of lavender. The black form was developed in 1919, followed by albinos and dark-eyed whites, and then the brown. One of the most recent additions to this group of friendly rabbits is the lilac, created during the 1980s. Recognizable by its white body and dark markings on the extremities, it is now becoming more common.

◆ BELOW
The Beveren has now been developed in a range of colours, but the attractive lavender variety, seen here, is the traditional form of the breed.

pure white in colour, with the pink eyes that confirm they are true albinos. Since the 1960s, two more colour forms have been developed – a black and a blue variety, both of which resemble the New Zealand in all respects apart from their coloration. Like the white New Zealand, the blue and black varieties are docile and placid. There is also a smaller breed called the New Zealand red, which has been developed in America. It is thought to be descended from crosses between Flemish giants and Belgian hares carried out in the early 1900s.

BELGIAN HARE
This slim, athletic, long-legged Belgian breed resembles a hare, but is nevertheless a rabbit. Its highly distinctive appearance caused a stir when it was first developed at the end of the 19th century. Early attempts at cross-breeding rabbits with hares

always proved futile, which confirms that the Belgian hare is in fact a pure rabbit. The coat is a deep chestnut colour with black shading. The long body means that it requires a tall hutch, to enable it to sit up on its hindquarters. It is active by nature, and this, coupled with its sleek appearance, makes it an attractive choice for a pet.

BEVEREN
The rabbit known as the Beveren also originates from Belgium, and was developed during the 1890s. Today, the breed is large, typically weighing up to 4.5 kg (10 lb), and has a distinctive mandolin-shaped body. The coat has

HOUSING IN THE GARDEN

◆ BELOW
Mount the hutch on legs to ensure the base
remains dry and to keep wild rabbits away from
your pet. Secure door fastenings are essential
to protect against foxes and other predators.

Rabbits can be kept outdoors throughout the year, although they must have a snug, draught-proof area to retreat to when the weather is bad. As rabbits need to feel secure, the hutch should be divided into two connecting sections, one with a solid door, the other with a front made of wire mesh. Many pet shops sell hutches, or alternatively you can build one yourself. When choosing a hutch, make sure that it is high enough for the rabbit to be able to sit up to its full height and stand without difficulty. Ideally, the hutch is connected directly to a run, which allows your rabbit to run around and exercise freely without the need for supervision.

Position the rabbit hutch in a sheltered spot, out of the direction of prevailing winds. Avoid an area beneath trees, as branches may break off and damage the hutch. The run may extend off one of the sides or from the back of the hutch, with a broad, gently sloping ladder giving easy access in to and out of it. A door, which can be securely closed (and preferably locked), should always be incorporated into the hutch design.

If you decide to make your own hutch, choose good materials. Thick plywood should be used for the covered part, with good quality roofing felt providing a barrier on top to keep the interior dry. Place sliding trays inside to make cleaning easier. Put these in the rabbit's sleeping quarters and cover them with a layer of coarse shavings, with hay on top.

The run needs to have wire on its underside, unless it is placed on concrete slabs, such as a patio. This will prevent your rabbit from tunnelling out, or a predator, such as a fox, from getting in. Especially if the run is not connected to the hutch, place it in the shade: rabbits exposed to hot sun can die rapidly from heat stroke. Incorporate a sheltered area in the run to be safe.

POSITIONING A RABBIT HUTCH OUTDOORS

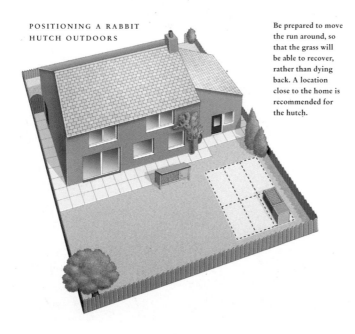

Be prepared to move the run around, so that the grass will be able to recover, rather than dying back. A location close to the home is recommended for the hutch.

CONSTRUCTING A RABBIT RUN

1 Building your own run for your rabbit can be cheaper than buying one, yet you will get a run of better quality. Start by preparing all the different components.

2 Power tools have greatly simplified the construction process, making it an easy task to prepare holes for the scews used to hold the run together.

3 A different fitment on the power tool will enable you to use it as a screwdriver, having drilled the holes first. Use stainless steel screws, which will not rust.

4 For some parts of the run, the timber will be better fixed together with nails. Always provide good support when nailing lengths of timber together.

5 When fixing the mesh on to the framework, use special netting staples for the purpose. Trim back any sharp ends of mesh, which could otherwise injure your rabbit.

6 Weatherproofing is essential, but it is safer to treat only the outer surfaces, where your rabbit will not gnaw the woodwork, to avoid any risk of poisoning.

7 Position the sides together carefully before drilling fixing holes, because any mistakes at this stage will be hard to rectify. You may want to use a clamp.

8 The run is now partially assembled, with just the other side section to fit into place. This will then anchor the structure together firmly.

9 Easy access to the run, so you can catch the rabbit without it being able to slip past you, is vital. Provide access by constructing doors in one of the sides.

10 If the run is to sit on grass rather than a solid base, cover the floor with mesh. Attach this along one edge and keep it taut.

11 Finally, fix bolts on to the doors. These should be well oiled to prevent them sticking and rusting up in the future.

12 *(right)* The completed run. This design provides sufficient height so that the rabbit can sit up on its hindquarters, and incorporates a dry retreat if the weather turns bad.

HOUSING IN THE HOME

House-rabbits have become very fashionable pets in recent years. One reason may be that, unlike cats and dogs, they do not require exercise outside and so they are ideal for city-dwellers. They can also be trained to use a litter tray. Most house-rabbit owners keep their pet in its hutch when they are out, and then allow it to run around the house when they are at home. This will help to prevent accidents, although some adjustments in the home will still be necessary.

PREPARING YOUR HOME

If you decide to keep a house-rabbit, you will need to follow a few practical safety measures in the home. A stair guard will be essential to protect the rabbit from accidents. You will also need to hide any exposed electrical cables, as a rabbit is more than likely to gnaw them. If you see your rabbit with a live cable in its mouth, switch off the power supply at the wall and disconnect the cable immediately. If the cable shows signs of damage, it will need to be replaced. Discourage the rabbit from nibbling at furniture and carpet by providing special rabbit chews. Ingested carpet fibres can cause a fatal intestinal obstruction if they are swallowed by the rabbit.

INDOOR HOUSING

Specially designed hutches are now available for rabbits living indoors. It is a good idea to fit a pen around the hutch for extra safety, and to keep your rabbit in its hutch or pen when you are out. Although it may seem appropriate to place the hutch and run

♦ ABOVE
A house-rabbit can prove to be as affectionate as a dog or cat in the home, and may be trained with surprising ease. The main problem is likely to be the rabbit's enthusiasm for nibbling.

♦ LEFT
Special indoor housing systems are available for house-rabbits, with this type of design giving your pet a clear view of its surroundings. An indoor hutch is another possibility.

in a conservatory or porch, bear in mind that the temperature here can rapidly rise to a fatal level for your rabbit on a hot day. Prepare the hutch in just the same way as outdoor accommodation. Do not forget to provide hay as this is an essential source of fibre in the rabbit's diet, and will lessen its inclination to chew at the carpets.

For house-training, choose a low-sided cat litter tray that gives the rabbit easy access, and use a lightweight litter. Scoop up some of the rabbit's droppings on to the litter, and then put the rabbit on the tray. It is often helpful to have a pen at this early stage as you can keep your pet confined here until it is trained in using the litter tray, and this will avoid any soiling around the home.

INDOOR SAFETY HAZARDS

Don't leave the doors to your home open, or your rabbit may run out.

Household plants can be dangerous for rabbits. Place them safely out of reach.

Rabbits like the warmth of the fire, but be sure they cannot singe their coats.

A kitchen is a very dangerous room for a rabbit, especially when you are cooking.

Keep electrical cables out of your rabbit's reach, disconnecting them if possible.

A washing machine can attract a rabbit, so keep the door firmly closed.

Furniture may be gnawed by your rabbit. Provide chews as a safe alternative.

FEEDING

Rabbits have an unusual digestive system, which means that they are susceptible to digestive upsets. This makes feeding your rabbit one of the most important aspects of its care.

DIGESTION

The rabbit's food will pass from the stomach to the small intestine and on to the caecum, a sac at the junction with the large intestine. Here, the rabbit does not have the enzymes needed to break down the cellulose present in plant cell walls, even though the bacteria in the caecum will break down the food. The absorption of nutrients takes place in the small intestine, and so in order to absorb cellulose the rabbit will pass the food out of its body, usually at night, in the form of soft pellets, and then consume them. This allows the nutrients to re-enter the digestive tract, passing to the small intestine, where they can be absorbed into the body.

Rabbit pellets

The most common digestive upset in rabbits is caused by a sudden change in diet. This means that the bacteria that play such a vital part in the rabbit's digestive process cannot adapt in time. Treatment with antibiotics is difficult because these drugs interfere with the functioning of the bacteria.

For this reason, it is essential to be aware of what food your new rabbit has been eating, and to keep to it for the first two or three weeks. Changes should be made gradually, with the new brand being introduced at the end

of the second week after the rabbit is rehomed. Mix the new food with the old, and increase the percentage of the new food over the next couple of weeks, to allow the rabbit's digestive system time to adjust to the change.

RABBIT FOODS

There are many different types of rabbit food on the market. Most mixes contain a variety of ingredients, such as cereals and pellets. Recent concerns over locust beans, which have been blamed for the death of some rabbits, have led to these being removed by some manufacturers. Check the labelling for the precise ingredients, and make a note of the "use-by" date for the vitamin and mineral content of the mix.

If your rabbit has not been used to fresh foods, introduce this carefully in small amounts. You can feed a rabbit a wide range of fresh foods, including dandelion, grass, carrots and cabbage.

◆ BELOW
A selection of food dishes and a water bottle. Food dishes chosen for rabbits must not be easy to tip over, or light enough to allow your pet to throw them around.

Rabbit mix

Bran mash

Vitamin supplement and mineral blocks

Always wash the food beforehand and make sure it is fresh. Many rabbits develop serious diarrhoea when they are first put in an outdoor run, because they are not used to eating grass. The consequences can be fatal, so it is important to acclimatize the rabbit to grass before it goes outside.

A rabbit that is fed a commercial formulated food is unlikely to need any supplements to its diet. Treats available from pet stores can be offered occasionally, but watch out for signs that your rabbit is overweight: pet rabbits can become obese, especially if they are fed a diet that is too concentrated. Aim to provide a balanced diet, matched to your pet's energy requirements. Rabbits kept outside need more food than those kept indoors. A neutered rabbit will also need less food.

Pet rabbits can be tamed to eat from the hand. Children need to be taught not to hold on to the food item for too long, however, because the rabbit will carry on nibbling and may then take a bite at their fingers.

◆ BELOW
A rabbit diet should consist of both fresh and dry foods. Make any dietary changes gradually to avoid digestive upsets.

Seed sticks

Rabbit biscuits

Carrots

Cabbage

Apples

19

GENERAL CARE

Rabbits can be nervous when they are first rehomed and it is important to get into the routine of picking up a young rabbit regularly so that it becomes accustomed to it. Always supervise a child attempting to pick up their pet for the first few weeks. Make sure that the child does not have bare arms as rabbits have sharp claws, which can cause painful scratches if they struggle. This applies especially in the case of young rabbits, whose claws are often especially needle-like. Although rabbits must never be picked up by their ears, holding these gently while supporting the body can quieten a rabbit that is proving difficult to restrain. Support the underside of the rabbit's body with one hand and use the other hand to hold its body, so that it will not leap

PICKING UP
A RABBIT
PROPERLY

1 *(left)* Gently restrain your rabbit by placing one hand on the side of its body and another under its hindquarters. Never pick a rabbit up by its ears.

2 *(left)* Then slide your hands under the body, providing support especially for the hindquarters.

out of your grasp. Once settled, rabbits rarely try to wriggle free, nor will they attempt to bite.

HYGIENE AND MAINTENANCE

You will need a suitable carrying container for your rabbit, particularly when you want to move it from its run back to its cage. Although you can use a strong cardboard box, a cat carrier will be more secure for longer journeys, such as trips to the vet.

Change the bedding in the rabbit's hutch at least once a week, and occasionally scrub out the hutch. Try to do this on a warm day, when the rabbit is in its run, which will allow the interior to dry quickly. You can use a special disinfectant recommended for this purpose. Check regularly on the back and undersides of the roof of the outdoor hutch for any leaks. A hole

♦ ABOVE
It helps to have a secure carrier so that you can move your rabbit safely from its hutch to the run.

in the roofing felt is the most likely reason, and this will need to be repaired before it becomes more serious. Do not treat the exterior woodwork of the hutch with a weather-proofing agent when the

rabbit is inside, as chemical fumes can be harmful. You should expect a well-maintained hutch to last for the rabbit's lifetime.

Gnawing of furniture and carpets can often be a problem inside the

house. Providing wooden blocks for your rabbit to gnaw on will help, or you can prepare dry crusts of wholemeal bread by roasting them in the oven. Allow the crusts to cool before offering them to your pet.

CLEANING OUT A RABBIT HUTCH

1 The hutch must be cleaned thoroughly at least once and possibly twice each week. A plastic dustpan and brush will be useful for this task, helping to remove the soiled bedding.

2 Having removed much of the soiled bedding, pull out the tray and tip the rest of the contents into a sack. This discarded material is ideal for composting.

3 When you decide to scrub out the interior, choose a sunny day when the rabbit is in its run, allowing the hutch to dry thoroughly before returning the rabbit here.

BREEDING

◆ BELOW
Young rabbits at three days of age. Note the
dark patches of skin which indicate that these
areas will have dark fur in due course. Avoid
any disturbance to the nest.

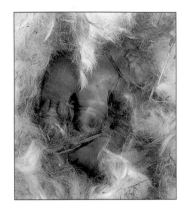

Rabbits have a justified reputation
for being prolific breeders, and it is
important not to let them breed
without having planned what you
are going to do with the offspring.

It is relatively straightforward to
sex rabbits once they are mature, from
about five months of age, when the
testes of the buck have descended into
the scrotum. Before this, a clear sign
will be that the gap between the anal
and genital openings will be longer in
the case of the buck, compared to the
doe. One of the reasons that rabbits
breed freely is that does do not have
a regular reproductive cycle resulting
in ovulation. They are unusual among
mammals, being "induced ovulators",
which means that it is the stimulus of

◆ BELOW
A Dutch rabbit with her young. In the case of
this pure-bred breed, the pattern of markings
is highly distinctive, with the white area on the
face being called a blaze.

mating which triggers the release of
eggs from the ovary. As a result, the
likelihood of fertilization occurring
is greatly increased.

It is not recommended to keep
bucks together as they can fight
viciously. Does are more likely to live
in harmony in spacious surroundings,
but it is not uncommon for bullying
to occur, with a doe proving to be
spiteful towards her companion.

MATING AND PREGNANCY

The larger breeds of rabbit can be
much slower to mature than their
smaller relatives. It may take up to
nine months for giant breeds to
become mature, which is twice as long
as it takes in the Dutch, dwarf or rex
breeds. The doe will be ready to mate
when the skin around her genitals
takes on a deep reddish hue, rather
than pink. At this stage, she can be
introduced to the buck, and mating is
likely to occur soon afterwards. It may
be better to leave the pair together for
a couple of days to be sure, and then
the doe can be transferred back to
her quarters.

Assuming that she is pregnant,
the doe will start to build a nest as
the time for giving birth approaches,
although in the first two weeks or
so, she will not appear to put on any
weight. This tends to occur towards
the end of pregnancy, and her mobility
is not unduly restricted in the early
stages. The doe will benefit from being
supplied with a kindling box, lined
with clean hay, where she can give
birth. Just beforehand, she will start
to pluck her fur to form a nest for her
offspring. Pregnancy in the rabbit lasts
approximately 31 days. Although as
many as 12 offspring may be born, a

typical litter comprises six to nine young, which are known as kittens. At birth, they have no hair, although dark fur markings, such as spots, will appear as blotches on the skin, which is otherwise pink. The kittens' ears are short in relation to their body size.

Development is rapid, with fur appearing after four days. The eyes open just over a week after birth. It is vital not to intrude into the nest, because your scent may cause the doe to abandon or even attack her offspring. A problem is most likely to be drawn to your attention by repeated calls from the young if they are not receiving enough food. The doe may be suffering inflammation of the mammary glands, known as mastitis, which will require urgent veterinary treatment.

HANDREARING

If you should have to handrear a litter of young rabbits, you will need to feed them on warm goat's milk, which is the nearest natural substitute to that of the doe. Use an eye dropper or a small syringe as a feeding tool, but always disinfect this between feeds. Unfortunately, the task of hand-rearing is made difficult by the fact that the doe transfers immunity to her offspring via her milk, and if this is denied to them, they are likely to succumb to minor infections. Young rabbits will normally be fully weaned at nine weeks.

◆ LEFT
A group of Dutch rabbits at 12 days old. Their ears are still quite short at this stage, compared with their bodies, which is a feature of all young rabbits.

◆ BELOW
By 30 days old, the young rabbits are starting to eat independently, and will soon be ready to be weaned. They can be tamed easily at this stage by being handled.

◆ ABOVE
Exhibition stock is usually rung in order to identify the rabbits individually. The ring on this rabbit cannot be removed without being cut off, as the leg will have grown too large.

◆ LEFT
The patterning of rabbits such as the Dutch does not vary as they grow older. These particular individuals are now 60 days old.

GROOMING AND SHOWING

Most rabbits need very little by way of coat care, but the angora, with its soft, long coat, needs daily grooming to prevent the coat from becoming tangled and matted. If left, mats will need be to cut out of the fur. Breeds derived from the angora require similar care. Use special grooming combs, which are sold for cats and dogs. These have rotating teeth that help to tease the fur apart, rather than pulling on the strands of hair.

During the summer months, it is vital to examine the underparts of a rabbit regularly for fur soiled through a digestive upset. If bluebottle flies lay eggs in or near the soiled fur, the maggots will bore into the body through the skin, releasing potentially fatal toxic compounds into the blood. A rabbit with fly strike, as this condition is known, will need urgent veterinary treatment to remove all the maggots and treat the infected area; otherwise, the rabbit will die. It may be necessary to keep the rabbit indoors until the infection has healed, to reduce the chance of it recurring.

♦ LEFT
The grooming requirements of individual breeds differ significantly, and this is a factor that you need to consider when choosing a rabbit. The angora, seen here, is a particularly demanding breed in terms of its grooming needs.

♦ LEFT
Considerable care has to be given to show rabbits like this angora, so that they look at their best when being judged. Competition at rabbit show events is invariably fierce.

♦ BELOW LEFT
The result of all that hard work – an immaculate angora rabbit. If it is not groomed, the fur quickly becomes matted.

CLAW CLIPPING

A pet rabbit's claws can become overgrown quite easily. This is especially dangerous for a rabbit that lives in the home as it can become caught up by its claws in upholstery or floor coverings. You can clip the claws back yourself, although a steady hand is needed, and this is not a job for young children. If in any doubt, your vet will be able to do it for you. You will need a proper pair of claw clippers, rather than ordinary scissors, which are likely to cause the nail to fray and split instead of cutting it cleanly off.

If clipping the claws yourself, first locate the blood supply to the claw, visible as a reddish streak. This may be difficult to detect in rabbits with dark claws, and if this is the case, you will need veterinary experience to prevent the claw from being cut too short and starting to bleed as a consequence. Should you see blood when you are clipping the claws at home, press a damp piece of clean cotton wool (cotton ball) to the wound.

SHOWING RABBITS

Rabbit shows at local and regional level are listed in newspapers and specialist publications and, if you are interested in one particular variety of rabbits, there may be a breed club that you can join as well. Rabbits are rung for exhibition purposes at about two months of age, before the ankle joint becomes too big for the ring to pass over it. Rings are produced in various sizes for different breeds and it may be necessary to band the smaller breeds at a slightly younger age. The breeder's details and the year of the rabbit's birth are encoded on the ring, which will normally remain in place throughout its life. Check the ring occasionally, however, to check that it moves freely on the leg and is not causing the rabbit any discomfort. If the ring needs to be removed for any reason, ask your vet do this for you. Ringing is not the only way to mark rabbits for identification, however. In many countries, tattooing is preferred.

◆ ABOVE LEFT
At a show, it can appear as if the rabbits are being compared with each other to find the winner. However, in reality, they are being judged against the breed standard.

◆ ABOVE RIGHT
It is vital that show rabbits are used to being handled, so that when being judged, as here, they will not struggle but remain relaxed.

◆ RIGHT
Rabbits are kept in pens before and after judging. Vaccination, especially against the rabbit disease VHD, is very important for show rabbits.

GUINEA PIGS

Guinea pigs are unusual among rodents in that they lack a tail. It is possible that, in evolutionary terms, the tail was deemed unnecessary because of the guinea pig's reluctance to climb. Taming is straightforward, especially if they are obtained when young, as guinea pigs will not attempt to bite when being picked up, making them an ideal choice of pet for children. Guinea pigs are also highly popular as exhibition subjects.

INTRODUCTION

◆ BELOW
The agouti colour form approximates most closely to that of the wild guinea pig.

Guinea pigs are members of the rodent family, forming part of a group known as the caviomorphs. They originate from the Andean region of South America, and were probably first domesticated by the Incas over 750 years ago. The wild ancestors of the guinea pig look very different to the colourful varieties kept today. Their coats show greyish agouti patterning, not unlike that of a wild rabbit, and provide them with a good level of camouflage.

It was not until the 1700s that guinea pigs were first brought to Europe. There are a number of different explanations for their unusual name. It could be that they were brought from the area of Guianas, which became corrupted to "Guinea", or it may have been because the first ships that carried them across the Atlantic ocean visited Guinea, on the west coast of Africa, before sailing north to Europe. Alternatively, there could be a financial explanation – these

rodents soon became immensely sought-after as pets, and it could be a reflection of the high value initially placed upon them in England, where they could fetch the princely sum of one guinea. It is easier to see why they became known as pigs. This is not just a reflection of

◆ LEFT
Camouflage is very important for the survival of guinea pigs in the wild, as they are surrounded by many potential predators.

◆ RIGHT
Young wild guinea pigs. Unlike many rodents, they are developed enough when born to move around freely.

While it is possible to keep
pet rabbits and guinea pigs housed
together, the rabbit may bully its
smaller rodent companion. If you
choose to have these pets sharing
accommodation, make sure that the
hutch is spacious, and select a smaller
breed of rabbit, which is less likely to
hurt the guinea pig if it accidentally
jumps on top of it. Separate them at
once if you notice signs of bullying.

Unlike some of the other rodent
species, there is no unpleasant odour
associated with guinea pigs.

their corpulent body shape, but also of
their "oinking" calls. Not surprisingly,
therefore, males are known as boars
while females are called sows.

Rather confusingly, guinea pigs
are also sometimes known as cavies,
which is a reflection of the name of
the group to which they belong –
the caviomorphs. This group is
characterized by the arrangement of
the muscles of their jaws, and also
their long gestation period, compared
with that of other rodents. As a result,
although they have fewer young, their
offspring are born in a relatively
advanced state of development.

GUINEA PIGS AS PETS
Guinea pigs make ideal pets for
children, particularly as they are small,
easy to handle and will not attempt
to bite when picked up. They can be
housed either in the home or outside
in a hutch throughout the year, even
in temperate areas. Even so, as with
rabbits, it is certainly not advisable
to buy a guinea pig that has been
kept in the relative warmth of a pet
store, and then transfer it immediately
to an outdoor hutch during the winter.

As household pets,
however, guinea pigs are
far shyer than rabbits.
They can be handled
easily since they do
not bite, but they are
likely to scurry away
under furniture for
long periods rather than
being content to remain
alongside you like a
rabbit. Under normal
circumstances, guinea pigs
will live for about six years.

SMOOTH-COATED BREEDS

◆ BELOW

A self black guinea pig. This individual is
showing reddish hairs in its coat, which would
spoil its exhibition potential; however, this will
not make it any less attractive to keep as a pet.

The smooth-coated guinea pigs are
nearer in appearance to their wild
ancestors than other varieties.
They are now sub-divided into two
categories – the self (single colour)
varieties, such as cream, chocolate
or black, and the patterned varieties,
such as the tortoiseshell.

SELF VARIETIES

The black is one of the most popular
members of the self group, thanks
to its glossy, sleek coat. For showing
purposes, it should be entirely black
in colour. Breeders regard any odd
white or even red hairs in its coat as a
serious show flaw. Even as they grow
older, these guinea pigs do not fade
in colour. The self chocolate is
another dark variety, the colour of
plain (semisweet) chocolate, with
similarly coloured dark eyes and ears.
Depth of coloration in the coat is
essential, as it is with all self-coloured
guinea pigs.

As new colours have been
developed, some of the older varieties
have declined in numbers. One of
these is the self red, which is an
attractive shade of rich mahogany
with ruby-red eyes. The coloration of
the self golden can sometimes almost

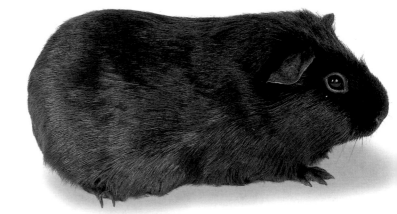

◆ ABOVE

Agouti coloration arises from the
fact that there is a series of dark
and light bands running down the
hairs. Some forms of the agouti
have red eyes.

◆ LEFT

Light shades within the self
category are very popular. This is a
self beige, a dilute form of the self
chocolate. The depth of coloration
should be seen over its entire body.

◆ LEFT
The coat texture
of the rex is very
distinctive, giving
these guinea pigs
a rather woolly
appearance. This
feature can be
combined with the
smooth, short coat
type, as here, or with
longer hair.

verge on red, although the preferred
shade is ginger. The eyes in this case
are usually pink, although there is
also a rarer dark-eyed form.

Lighter shades in the self-coloured
group include the cream, and a darker
form that has a much yellower
appearance, known as the self buff.
The cream is sometimes known as
the "champagne cavy" to describe
the shade of colour required for show
stock, with paler coloration being
preferred. Self white guinea pigs are
often slightly smaller than other
colours, especially the true albino,
which is recognizable by its red rather
than dark eyes. The stipulation here
is for the coat colour to be pure
white, with no trace of a yellowish
hue. These white guinea pigs should
not be confused with the Himalayan
form, which is also pure white, but
is distinguishable by the darker
chocolate or black areas on the nose
and ears. The chocolate is the lighter
form of the two Himalayan varieties.

New self colours are still being
evolved as the demand for novelty
shades grows. The self blue – a
bluey shade of grey – which has
been developed in the United States,
marks a significant departure from
existing solid guinea pig colours.

PATTERNED VARIETIES

The tortoiseshell and white is a
striking example of a short-coated,
patterned guinea pig, with black,
white and red patches in its coat.
The Dutch form of the guinea pig
bears a strong resemblance in its
patterning to the rabbit of the same
name; the coloured and white areas
must be clearly defined for showing.
Darker colours, such as red or black,
are preferred, because these create
a more evident contrast in the coat,

but other colours are seen, even agouti
Dutch combinations. Agouti markings
result from light and dark banding
running down each individual hair.

The more recently developed
varieties include the Dalmatian,
so-called because its black and
white spotted patterning is
reminiscent of the dog breed, while
roans are distinguished by an even
distribution of coloured and white
areas throughout their coats. Roans
can be bred in various colours.

◆ BELOW
Coat patterning is an important feature
of certain guinea pig varieties. The three
tortoiseshell and white, short-coated
individuals shown here are siblings.

LONG-HAIRED AND REX COATS

ABYSSINIAN

For many years the Abyssinian and Peruvian breeds were the only long-haired guinea pigs recognized. The Abyssinian has a coat comprising a series of rosettes and ridges. The rosettes do not overlap but, where the hair extends out around the edge of the rosette to meet another rosette, a ridge is formed. There should ideally be four symmetrical rosettes running down the sides of the body, and a similar number along the back. In fact, the coat of the Abyssinian should not lie flat at any point over its entire body. The individual hairs themselves are quite short, measuring no more than 4 cm (1½ in) long.

As the wiry-haired coat of the Abyssinian is genetically dominant over short-coated cavies, if these are paired together, the offspring will have rosettes, but these are usually not as well defined as the rosettes seen in a true Abyssinian lineage. In this way, however, new self colours can be introduced to the Abyssinian breed. Even so, self reds and self blacks, as well as brindles, tortoiseshells and roans, are the most common colour forms of the Abyssinian because their

♦ TOP
A self red Abyssinian. This breed is characterized by the lie of its coat. In this particular case, the fur must be entirely red, displaying no trace of white hairs.

♦ ABOVE
Bi-colours exist in the case of the Abyssinian, as shown by this gold and white individual.

♦ BELOW
The rex mutation gives a coarser texture to the fur. This is a silver agouti example.

hair texture is often better. It can take up to 18 months for their coats to develop to their full extent.

PERUVIAN

Because of the Peruvian's demanding grooming requirements, it is not recommended as a pet, except for the most dedicated owner. The young are born with a short coat, but by adulthood it can reach 50 cm (20 in) or more in length. As the coat mats very easily, the Peruvian is not kept on hay, which can become entangled in the coat. Instead, the hay should be supplied in a hayrack.

SHELTIE

The sheltie is the long-haired form of the smooth-coated guinea pigs, and is instantly distinguishable from the Peruvian by its fur, which lies flat and is not swept forwards over its head, and the absence of a parting extending

◆ LEFT
Grey agouti and cream Abyssinian. The agouti
characteristic is shown by the dark and light
banding extending down the individual hairs,
creating a sparkling appearance.

CRESTED MUTATION

Another characteristic, linked with a wide range of colours, is the crested mutation. The crest itself should be even in size and circular in shape, being located just in front of the ears. In the case of the English crested mutation, the crest matches that of the surrounding fur, but it is always white in the case of the American crested. When combined with the texel, the crested has given rise to the form known as the alpaca.

down the back. The satin characteristic has been introduced to these long-haired guinea pigs, and this has ensured that their coats do not lose their lustre as they grow older. In other cases, the satin characteristic highlights the natural gloss of the coat.

◆ BELOW
The crested characteristic can be combined with any colour. In the American form, seen here, it is always white.

REX MUTATIONS

The rex mutation is a relatively new variant, but has become very popular both in Europe and North America, where it is often described as a teddy. The rex's fur is slightly curly and very coarse to the touch. It is a recessive mutation, so rex guinea pigs must be paired together to produce rex offspring. The rex has now been bred in a very wide range of colours. It has also been possible to combine it with the sheltie to create the texel, which has a curly but shorter coat than the true sheltie. The merino is the result of crosses between the rex and the Peruvian guinea pigs.

◆ BELOW
A family of tortoiseshell and white rex guinea pigs. Note the favoured white blaze extending down the nose between the eyes. Individual markings are variable.

HOUSING IN HOME AND GARDEN

Guinea pigs are less destructive than some of the other rodent species, but it is to be expected that they will gnaw at woodwork within their hutch, often concentrating on one particular spot.

OUTDOOR HOUSING

Hutches outdoors should be divided into two sections – an outer area with a mesh front, and secure, snug sleeping quarters. Guinea pigs do not sit up like rabbits, so the hutch does not need to be especially tall. When you buy a hutch check that the doors are secure, and add combination locks to latches to deter dexterous foxes. It is also a good idea to oil the hinges every couple of months, enabling them to open smoothly and helping to prolong their lifespan.

Regularly check the roofing felt to ensure that the interior remains dry. A dense layer of hay will help to provide warm sleeping quarters, and will supplement the guinea pig's diet. If you are planning to construct the hutch yourself, you should give it

♦ RIGHT
An indoor enclosure for a guinea pig, complete with a water bottle. The base prevents bedding from being scattered in the room. Note the removable mesh lid, protecting the guinea pig from any dogs and cats also sharing your home.

secure legs, made of 5 cm (2 in) square timber, that stand at least 30 cm (1 ft) off the ground. The sides of the hutch can be constructed using tongue-and-groove timber, although thick marine plywood often proves to be more durable. The roof should slope from front to back, with an overhang at the back so that rainwater runs off readily, rather than down the back of the hutch where it would rot the wood.

Outdoor runs for guinea pigs are similar to rabbit runs, although, like hutches, they do not need to be as tall.

Pet stores usually stock a variety of runs, including ark-shaped designs, which have a dry section at one end where the guinea pig can retreat in bad weather, and rectangular runs, which also have a covered area. Check that you can reach right into the run to pick up the guinea pig, since guinea pigs can be very difficult to catch.

Position the run in a shady spot and remember to move it every week or so, to ensure that the area of grass beneath the sides of the run does not die back. Avoid using lawn that has recently been treated with weedkillers or potentially harmful chemicals. Place the run on level ground as a guinea pig may otherwise escape beneath one of the sides; you may not be aware of this danger if the grass is long. Fresh drinking water should always be available in the run.

INDOOR HOUSING

An indoor hutch should combine a cage with a plastic base and a wire mesh surround that prevents the guinea pig from clambering out. The base will ensure that bedding is not scattered out into the room. Wire mesh lids, which clip on to the hutch, prevent attacks from dogs and cats.

♦ LEFT
Outdoor guinea pig hutches need to be well constructed from durable materials, with a covering of heavy-duty roofing felt to keep the interior dry. You may need to reinforce the door fitments to keep your pet safe.

MAKING A GUINEA PIG HUTCH

1 Start by cutting all of the components to size. These may then be glued in place, using a non-toxic adhesive. Leave to dry.

2 Clamps will help to hold the glued surface to the adjacent area until it has dried. Holes can then be drilled as necessary.

3 Power tools will often simplify the assembly process. The screws themselves should fit snugly into the holes.

4 Here the sections are being assembled. The wooden supports are on the outside of the hutch, out of the guinea pig's reach.

5 The door hinges are an important part of the hutch. Do not economize here, as they may otherwise start rusting prematurely.

6 The assembled hutch, apart from the roof unit. Trim off any sharp edges of mesh on the door frame, so that they cannot injure your pet.

7 Apply the roofing felt. Note how the roof of the hutch is broader than the interior to ensure a better fit.

8 Fold over the roof felt at each of the corners, once the required length has been cut off the roll. Take care not to damage it at this stage.

9 Broad-headed clout nails are needed to attach the roofing felt. Check that this is taut as otherwise it may be ripped off in a strong wind.

10 The roof section can then be fitted on top of the hutch. Screws fitted through the sides into the inner supports provide anchorage.

11 Bolts to keep the hutch door securely closed can be fitted next. These will make it difficult for a predator to reach the guinea pig.

12 *(right)* The cage must be kept off the ground, with legs being fitted to the base, along with supporting struts. This ensures that the interior will stay dry during bad weather. You may want to add sliding trays on the floor, so that it will be easier to clean the interior simply by pulling these out. They need to fit snugly over the floor area.

13 Treat the exterior sides, legs and underside of the hutch with a non-toxic wood preservative, and allow this to dry before placing the guinea pig into its new home.

FEEDING

◆ BELOW
A bottle brush will be required to clean the
guinea pig's drinker at least once a week,
preventing it becoming green on the sides
as the result of algal growth.

Guinea pigs have an unusual metabolic quirk, shared with humans beings and marmosets but no other mammals. They are unable to manufacture Vitamin C from their food, and it must therefore be present in their diet if a deficiency is not to occur. As a result, complete foods for guinea pigs are supplemented with appropriate levels of this vital vitamin. Even if you are housing a rabbit and guinea pig together, it is very important to feed your guinea pig formulated food. A deficiency of Vitamin C causes a condition known as scurvy, resulting in dry, crusty skin and hair loss. Since

◆ BELOW
Guinea pigs need to be fed each day, with their dry food being provided in a heavy container that they cannot tip over easily. Change the drinking water at the same time.

scurvy can be confused with mite infestations, you should seek veterinary advice if the guinea pig shows these symptoms.

In addition to a prepared food, a guinea pig will readily eat a wide variety of greenstuff and vegetables. Broccoli and other brassicas, and spinach all contain relatively high levels of Vitamin C. Spinach is especially useful in the winter, when other sources of greenfood, such as dandelion leaves, are hard to find. Root vegetables, such as carrots, can also be offered regularly, particularly during the winter months.

Like rabbits, guinea pigs rely heavily on bacteria and protozoa in their large intestine to break down plant material, consuming their

♦ LEFT
Guinea pigs need a varied diet, and should not be offered dry food alone. They require a range of vegetables and other greenstuff if they are to remain in good health. Do not be surprised to find that they will nibble at bedding hay as well.

own droppings to obtain maximum nutritional benefit from their food. This means that you should not change your guinea pig's diet suddenly, but should make changes gradually, over a couple of weeks. It will not matter if you do not offer the same type of greenstuff each day, but it is harmful not to offer such foods for a period and then allow the guinea pig into a run where it will gorge itself on grass.

Always feed your guinea pig every day, and provide fresh water as well. It may help to provide the fresh food in a feeding bowl, rather than simply dropping it in the bedding where it can be harder to clear up and can possibly turn mouldy.

A range of treats is available for guinea pigs, but one addition to the diet traditionally favoured by guinea pig keepers is a bran mash. This is made by mixing bran with a little warm water and is especially valued during the winter months. Mix just enough to be eaten in a day, removing the food container when your pet has eaten and washing it out thoroughly.

There are a number of plants that are potentially poisonous for guinea pigs, and these should never be fed to your pet. Avoid bulbous plants, bracken and ragwort (*Senecio*). Among the more common garden weeds, both buttercups (*Ranunculus*) and convolvulus (*Convolvulus*) are toxic. The dangers posed by garden plants are usually listed in horticultural catalogues. Foxgloves (*Digitalis*) and lily-of-the-valley (*Convallaria*), as well as rhododendron (*Rhododendron*), should also be avoided.

Guinea pig mix

Bran mash

Broccoli

GENERAL CARE

It can be rather unnerving to hold a guinea pig for the first time as it may squeal as if in pain, and this can be especially alarming for a child. However, this shouldn't happen if you are gentle, and once your guinea pig is used to being handled regularly it will usually stop making this noise. Since guinea pigs do not bite instinctively, they can be picked up easily, although they will often try to avoid capture.

HANDLING
To pick up your guinea pig, place your left hand in front of it as it runs around its hutch, with your right hand behind it. Use your right hand to restrain the guinea pig by placing your fingers around its body. If you are left-handed, it may be easier to reverse your grip. Having caught the rodent, slide your hand under its hindquarters, and lift it up out of its hutch. Once it is held in this way, the guinea pig will generally not struggle, but take care not to loosen your grip at this stage because if you do drop it accidentally it is likely to be seriously injured in the fall.

TRANSPORTING YOUR PET
Use a sturdy cardboard box or pet carrier for transporting your guinea pig. Check the flaps on the base of the box to ensure that it is strong enough. Reinforce the base with packaging tape, and, as a further precaution, support the box from

PICKING UP A GUINEA PIG

1 By scooping your hand under the guinea pig's body, you will stop your pet from being able to run away. Do not be alarmed if the guinea pig squeaks – this is its warning call to others.

2 As you start to lift the guinea pig off the ground, slide your other hand beneath its abdomen to provide support for its hindquarters. Take particular care if the guinea pig is pregnant.

beneath with your hands. If you place some hay in the box, the guinea pig will burrow comfortably and will not panic. It is not likely to gnaw its way out of the box if housed here only for a short time, but never leave it where cats or dogs could gain access to it.

GUINEA PIG HYGIENE
The hutch should be cleaned out thoroughly at least once a week, with the bedding making ideal compost.

♦ ABOVE
Once it realizes that it will not be hurt when picked up, a guinea pig will lie comfortably in this position. This is a male, known as a boar.

Always keep a close watch on your guinea pig's droppings because these give a vital insight into its state of health, and they can be particularly significant in the case of older boars. In later life, boars are especially susceptible to a condition known as rectal impaction, when the muscular contractions necessary to force the faeces out of the anus become weak, causing the droppings to accumulate. This results in a painful swelling at the end of the digestive tract.

The problem will be apparent if the guinea pig is examined from beneath. Although it is a highly unpleasant task for both parties, the only solution will be to pour olive oil carefully into the anus and then gently massage the obstruction out wearing disposable gloves (your vet will do this for you if you prefer). A general purpose dietary supplement may be needed to prevent further deterioration.

WINTER CARE OUTDOORS
During the colder winter months, it is a good idea to bring the hutch into a sheltered, well lit outbuilding. If you leave the guinea pig outside, be sure that it has enough bedding to stay warm and check it daily. Check also that there is an adequate supply of drinking water available. It is not

recommended to use an earthenware bowl for this purpose, because it will quickly become fouled with bedding. A better option is to use a bottle that can be attached to the outside of the cage. Take precautions with this system if the temperature is set to drop below freezing point: do not fill the bottle to the top or when the water expands, as it changes into ice, it may crack the bottle. Check also that the stainless steel spout is free from ice, as this will stop the flow of water. Squeezing the bottle when it is full is the best way of checking for a blockage.

♦ BELOW
Take care when carrying guinea pigs in this way that they do not become scared, wriggle free and fall to the ground.

BREEDING

It is potentially dangerous to wait until a guinea pig sow is a year old before allowing her to have a litter. As the sow grows older, her pelvic bones will fuse together, and they will not expand easily to allow for the passage of young through the birth canal. This means that the risk of the young being trapped and having to be born by a Caesarean section is greatly increased. The ideal time for a sow to be mated for the first time is between five and six months of age. The stretching of the bones and muscles that takes place within the pelvis is then permanent, so that future litters born later in life are unlikely to result in a sow experiencing a difficult birth, which is known as dystocia.

Males mature even earlier and are able to mate successfully at only one month old. It is necessary, therefore, to separate males from females at an early stage, although it is usual to wait until the age of four months or so before using males for stud purposes.

Sexing of guinea pigs is reasonably straightforward. With a boar, gentle pressure either side of the genital opening will bring the penis into view. In the case of sows, there is usually a membrane over this orifice. Breeding is straightforward, with the female being placed in the male's quarters. More than one sow can be housed successfully with a boar, provided that the hutch is sufficiently large. Sows come into season approximately every 16 days, so that leaving a pair together for about five weeks should give adequate time for mating to take place.

The sow should then be transferred back to separate quarters to give birth. You can usually tell if a female is pregnant about six weeks after mating occurred, as the movements of the foetuses will be clearly discernible from this stage onwards. Do not squeeze her body to detect the offspring though, as this could inflict serious damage on them. A dietary supplement of Vitamin C may be useful during pregnancy, when the sow will double her requirement for this important vitamin.

The young are born – very often during the night – after a gestation period of approximately 63 days. Around this period, you may not know with any certainty if the young have been born. Take particular care when opening the hutch door to the sleeping quarters for an inspection, to prevent any newborn babies tumbling down on to the floor.

CARING FOR THE YOUNG

Baby guinea pigs are miniature adults, fully developed at birth, with their eyes already open. They may be somewhat darker in colour, however, and, in the case of long-haired breeds, they will have much shorter fur. A typical litter is made up of three or four offspring, but if the litter is much larger, keep a close watch on the female for signs of a serious

◆ LEFT
Young Himalayan guinea pigs are predominantly white in colour at birth. The darker markings on their bodies will develop with age.

◆ BELOW
A female tortoiseshell and white Abyssinian with her litter. Note the variability in their markings.

condition known as pregnancy toxaemia. Typical signs include loss of appetite and twitching, followed by convulsions. Obese sows are the most at risk. Rapid veterinary treatment will be needed if the sow is to recover.

Young guinea pigs are born in an advanced state of development, which means that they can eat solid food almost immediately, although they still benefit greatly from their mother's milk. If a litter is orphaned, supplementary feeding is not so critical to their survival. They can be handreared on evaporated milk, diluted with two parts of cooled boiled water, and mixed with a cereal baby food and a vitamin supplement.

♦ BELOW
The grooming requirements of the different
breeds of guinea pig differ significantly. Long-
haired breeds, such as the coronet shown here,
must be groomed every day.

GROOMING AND SHOWING

The grooming requirements of guinea
pigs vary greatly from minimal to
fairly heavy, depending on whether
your pet is long- or short-haired. To
keep a pet guinea pig tidy and clean,
you will need to make sure there is no
food or bedding material lodged in its
fur. If you have a long-haired guinea
pig, you will also need to give the coat
a regular brush to keep it free of
tangles and mats.

SHOW PREPARATION
If you want to show your guinea pig,
you will need to make some finishing
touches before the show to make sure
it looks its best.

With a Peruvian guinea pig, you
will need to train its hair, using brown
paper strips and small blocks of balsa
wood, from the age of three months.
This helps to encourage the sweep of
the hair, which, for the purpose of
the show, extends over all parts of the
guinea pig's body, including the head.
The wrappers, which are like hair
curlers, are folded in a concertina

shape with the balsa block held inside
and kept in place with rubber bands.
Each wrapper measures 15 cm (6 in) in
width, with the balsa block being 5 cm
(2 in) wide and 2.5 cm (1 in) across.
In the case of young Peruvian guinea
pigs, wrappers are placed first on the
sweep at the tail end and on each side
of the body, with further wrappers
being added as the guinea pig grows
older and its coat develops.

Preparing an Abyssinian guinea pig
for a show will involve brushing the
animal with a toothbrush, using a
brush with natural bristles, to avoid
introducing static to the animal's coat.
Brushing in this way will emphasize
the rosettes and ridges that are so
characteristic of the Abyssinian's coat.

AT THE SHOW
When it comes to judging, Peruvian
guinea pigs are placed on a special
judging stand – a hessian- (burlap-)
covered platform measuring 45 cm
(18 in) square and standing 15 cm
(6 in) off the ground – to display their
magnificent coats in all their finery.
With any exhibition guinea pig,
it will be necessary to train it to
stand still while being judged.
Guinea pig shows are held
often, although they are rarely
advertized outside the pages of

♦ LEFT
A Peruvian guinea pig being
prepared for a show. It is standing
on the typical hessian-covered
show stand.

◆ BELOW
Guinea pigs in their show pens. Advertisements
of such events can be found in the specialist
press, as well as club newsletters, usually giving
the address of the show secretary.

specialist publications. Even if you are not exhibiting, it is interesting to visit a show and see the many varieties of gunea pig that now exist. This is also a good place to meet breeders, who will often have stock for sale.

If you are interested in exhibiting your guinea pig, attending shows provides an opportunity to see what the judges are looking for. This will give you a much clearer idea than trying to visualize what is required by reading show standards and pouring over pictures in books. At both local and national shows, there may not be only guinea pigs on view, but also other small mammals, such as rabbits, rats and other rodents.

If you are wanting to see the rarer colour varieties of guinea pig, you will need to visit the bigger national events. If you are interested in exhibiting your own pet, however, it will be better to start out at local level, by joining a club in your area, before progressing to larger events with stronger competition.

◆ RIGHT
A group of smooth-coated guinea pigs being judged. The temporary spots on their ears correspond to their pen numbers, enabling individuals to be identified easily.

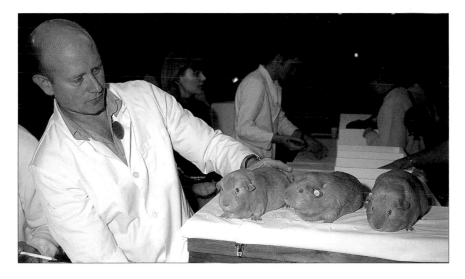

Hamsters

These small rodents are very popular throughout the world. They are bred in a range of colours and coat types, yet they still retain the rather nocturnal instincts of their ancestors, sleeping through most of the day. Bear in mind that hamsters are anti-social by nature, especially the Syrian or golden hamster, and they must be housed on their own. Hamsters make good children's pets, and they can be handled, although they may bite occasionally.

INTRODUCTION

Hamsters are a group of mainly small rodents with a wide distribution throughout the Old World. The common hamster (*Cricetus cricetus*) is the biggest member of the group, measuring 33 cm (13 in) in length and weighing approximately 475 g (17 oz). It is found in parts of Europe, where its numbers have declined significantly over recent years.

The appeal of hamsters as pets is relatively recent, and dates back to the capture of a female Syrian hamster (*Mesocricetus auratus*) and her young, in a field on a mountainside near Aleppo in Syria, in 1930. It was hoped that they could shed some light on a parasitic blood disease

◆ LEFT
Only when they are young can Syrian hamsters be housed together safely. They are otherwise likely to fight severely, even when introduced for mating, which needs to be closely supervised as a result.

◆ LEFT
The coat of the dwarf Russian, hamster becomes white in the winter.

but, before they could be taken to the University of Jerusalem, a number of the family had escaped and could not be recaptured.

The group that remained proved to be quite prolific, however, and before long these hamsters were sent to both the United States and the United Kingdom. Again, they bred well, and ultimately stock from London Zoo was passed to private breeders.

This marked the start of the hamster's rise to popularity as a pet, and the first hamster club was formed in the United Kingdom in 1945. However, this was not the first time that

Syrian hamsters had been kept
in Britain. In the late 1880s,
the former British Consul in Syria had
returned to the United Kingdom with
a breeding colony, but this ultimately
died out during the 1920s.

When they were first introduced
to the public, these hamsters were
described as golden hamsters because
of the golden colour of their coat.
Today, this name has become less
appropriate as a wide range of
colour varieties has been developed.
Now they are better known as
Syrian hamsters, which also helps to
distinguish them from the Russian and
Chinese hamsters. The Russian forms
in particular have grown greatly in
popularity over recent years, partly as
a result of their more sociable natures.
They, too, are now being bred in
different colours and coat types.

The dwarf Russian hamster
(Phodopus sungoris) occurs in the
eastern part of that country, and in
two different forms. The most striking
feature of the dwarf winter white
(P. s. sungoris) is its coat, which
changes colour, as its name suggests,
before the onset of winter, losing its
colour pigment and turning white.
This form originates from Siberia and
northern Kazakhstan, whereas the
dwarf Campbell's Russian hamster
(P. s. campbelli) ranges as far east as

northern China. This hamster, which
was not discovered until 1905, is
closely related to the winter white.
Both forms are also known as
Djungarian hamsters.

The third dwarf hamster from
this part of the world is Roborovski's
hamster (P. roborovskii), whose home
is the desert area of Mongolia. It can
be distinguished easily by the lack of
a dark stripe down its back. All three
forms of dwarf hamster have only
been widely available to pet-seekers
since the 1980s.

The Chinese hamster (Cricetulus
griseus) is less commonly kept than
the other breeds, and is therefore
less widely available. This hamster is
distinguishable from other breeds by
the length of its tail, which measures
about 2 cm (¾ in). These hamsters
originate from northern China, and
have a dark stripe down their back.
The coat itself is shorter and sleeker
than that of the Russian dwarf.

On average, a pet hamster can be
expected to live for between two
and three years.

◆ LEFT
In spite of their
size, dwarf Russian
hamsters are very
active by nature,
and will appreciate
having a special
hamster wheel in
their quarters for
exercise purposes.

SPECIES AND BREEDS

A wide range of colours have now been developed for the Syrian hamster, and an increasing number are emerging in the Russian species in particular. The wide choice of colours has helped to increase the hamsters' popularity with fanciers.

SYRIAN FORMS

The original golden form of the Syrian has a golden coat with black ticking on the individual hairs. The underparts are a contrasting shade of ivory white, and the ears are dark grey. There is also a darker golden form, with more extensive ticking and black ears, as well as a dilute form known as the light golden. The latter has no ticking on the coat and pure white underparts.

Among the other colours that have now been created is an attractive cream form, available in red-, ruby- and black-eyed variants. The yellow resembles the black-eyed cream, but can be distinguished by its darker coloration, which produces tipping on the guard hairs. The honey is very similar to the yellow, but can be easily distinguished by its paler ears and red eyes. The most colourful form of hamster is the cinnamon, which has orange-coloured fur.

◆ LEFT
For many years, the Syrian hamster was known as the golden hamster, thanks to its attractive flaxen coloration. As more colour varieties became established, so its name changed.

◆ LEFT
The Syrian hamster will sit up sometimes when it is eating or, as here, when it is looking around its environment.

◆ BELOW LEFT
Hamsters will use their forepaws like hands for eating and grooming purposes. This adds to their appeal as cute pets.

◆ BELOW RIGHT
It is not just the coloration of the Syrian hamster that has changed as a result of domestication. This is the long-coated or teddy form.

The three different forms of white Syrian hamster are distinguished by the pigmentation of their eyes and ears. The albino is a pure red-eyed white with no colour pigment present, in contrast to the dark-eared form.

The third form is the black-eyed white, recognizable by its black eyes and pink ears. All three forms have a pure snow white coat. Several grey forms of the Syrian hamster are also now established, as well as the dove,

The most distinctive colour of
the dwarf campbell's is the argente,
which has a ginger-coloured coat and
a chocolate-coloured stripe down its
back. There is also a true albino form,
which is entirely white in colour,
with the characteristic pink eyes.
A satin-coated mutation has also been
developed in recent years, and, as the
name suggests, this variety boasts a
noticeably sleek coat.

which has a lilac tinge to its colour.
Among other darker shades are the
chocolate, which is brown in colour,
and a new pure black variety.

In addition, there are a range of
marked colour varieties. These include
the banded, which has a white area
encircling the body, in combination
with any solid colour. Less rigorously
defined in terms of markings is the
variegated, with white and coloured
areas in its coat. The spotted is similar,
but in this case the markings are
circular. There is also a tortoiseshell
form, with yellow or black and brown
markings, which can also be combined
with white.

The potential for different hamster
varieties is enhanced by the various
coat types, which have been developed
to supplement the standard short-
haired form. The satin mutation can
be combined with this to make the
coat more shiny than normal. There

◆ BELOW
Syrian hamsters are being bred with specific
markings. The tortoiseshell and white, seen
here, has variable colour markings.

are also long-haired Syrian hamsters,
often known as teddies, and rexes,
distinguished by their curly coats.

RUSSIAN COLOUR FORMS
Of the dwarf Russian, one of the first
colours to be created was the sapphire.
This is bluish-grey with a stripe along
its back and blue markings. The pearl,
which is greyish in colour, has become
popular in recent years.

CHINESE HAMSTER
The best-known colour variant of
the Chinese hamster is the dominant
spot, which displays one or more
white spots on its body. A white
patch on the head is also favoured as
a requirement for exhibition stock.
Still rare is the white form of the
Chinese hamster, which is recognized
by the dark stripe running down the
length of its back.

◆ LEFT
The colour of dwarf
Russian hamsters may
change through the
year. Their dark fur
will be replaced by
white at the start of
the winter.

◆ RIGHT
In spite of their large
eyes, hamsters do not
have good vision. They
rely very heavily on
their sense of smell.

HOUSING AND FEEDING

Looking after your hamster correctly involves providing it with adequate food and shelter. These basics will ensure that it stays healthy and happy throughout its life.

HAMSTER CAGES

Although the traditional hamster cage is still a popular option, other more inventive housing systems are now available. If you opt for a cage, check that the base fits securely to the mesh roof area. Should there be any weakness here, the hamster is likely to find a gap and escape into the room. This applies especially in the case of young Russian hamsters, since cages on the market are generally intended for the larger Syrian species.

Another important aspect of cage design to consider is the strength of the door. It will be easier to take your hamster out of its quarters if the door is on the side of the cage, rather than in the roof. Door hinges have a tendency to become weaker over time, so it is a good idea to invest in a small combination padlock as an extra security precaution.

A cage should have a sleeping area. Make sure the bedding is safe hamster bedding, which will not cause a potentially fatal blockage in the rodent's intestinal tract if swallowed. You can buy bedding at a pet store. Tease it out by hand, so that the hamster can burrow into it easily.

Another option is sectional housing, which mimics the layout of a hamster's burrow in the wild, and has specially designed tunnel systems with enlarged nest areas. It is a good idea to begin with a basic starter kit, and then add inexpensive extra sections. You can create an entire housing system this way, with the water bottle fitting into the design. Such systems provide a more secure environment for a

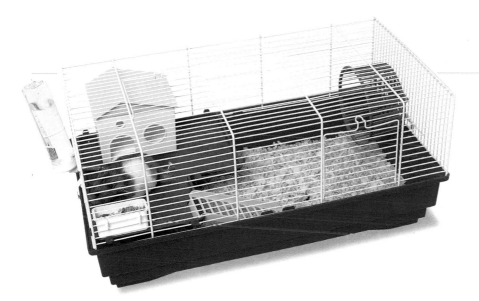

◆ LEFT
A typical hamster cage. Always check the door fastening is secure, because if a hamster escapes into the room, recapturing it is likely to prove very difficult.

hamster than a cage, but you should still check regularly to see that the rodent is not nibbling at the plastic at any one point, through which it might attempt to escape.

HAMSTER FOODS

Hamster mixes are readily available from pet stores. These will usually contain a variety of cereal seeds, as well as sunflower seeds and peanuts. These oil seeds should be offered in small quantities because of their high fat content, which can lead to obesity if they form the bulk of the hamster's diet. Commercial pelleted diets are

also available, although these tend to be the more expensive option. Use a small, heavyweight earthenware pot as a food bowl and provide fresh drinking water in a bottle, attached to the side of the hamster's quarters.

Do not forget to offer a little fresh food, such as a piece of sweet apple or greenstuff, on a daily basis as well. This can occasionally be sprinkled with a special small-animal vitamin and mineral supplement as an additional tonic. It is very important to match the amount of food offered to the hamster to the quantity being eaten because, otherwise, a hamster is likely

to waste food, carrying it back to its nest in its cheek pouches. Hamsters instinctively hoard food in this way, building up large supplies in their burrows when food is scarce above ground. Take particular care with fresh food, because this is likely to rot if left in the bedding material for a couple of days. It's a good idea to check the bedding regularly as this is likely to be harmful to your pet's health.

There are also a number of commercial treats now available to supplement your hamster's diet. These are useful for taming purposes, and can be offered directly by hand.

Feeding bowl

Mineral block

Hamster mix

GENERAL CARE AND BREEDING

It is important to provide a range of other items apart from food and water to ensure your hamster's well-being. Chews of various types will help to keep your hamster's incisor teeth in trim, although short branches cut from apple trees – which have not been sprayed with chemicals – can serve the same purpose. Crusts of bread, roasted in the oven, can be a valuable addition to the diet as well.

EXERCISE

It is vital to keep your hamster fit. In the wild, hamsters emerge from their burrows under cover of darkness, and may travel several miles in search of food or a mate. An exercise wheel will give your pet hamster a substitute for this night-time activity. Modern closed-wheel designs are the safest option, as a hamster could slip and injure itself in an open-weave wheel. Check regularly that the wheel is firmly in position and will not collapse on the hamster. Oil the wheel from time to time; it may be noisy when in use and, if the cage is in a child's bedroom, the wheel can disturb a sleeping child. Pregnant females seem to use a wheel most, and it may be that this helps to tone up their muscles in preparation for the birth of their pups.

♦ ABOVE
Syrian hamsters especially will benefit from having an exercise wheel. A closed wheel as shown is the safest option. Oil the wheel occasionally so that it moves freely.

♦ BELOW
A wide range of other toys are now available for hamsters. Being burrowing creatures by nature, they need adequate retreats of various types in their quarters.

Hamster play area

Sectional unit

Hamster nest

◆ BELOW
A male Syrian hamster. Note the scrotal swellings. Males can also be recognized by the relatively longer gap between their anal and genital openings.

◆ BELOW
A female, showing a much shorter ano-genital gap. In addition, females have a smoother rear profile when viewed from the side, compared with that of the males.

MATING AND PREGNANCY

Pairings of Syrian hamsters need to be carried out very cautiously to prevent injuries caused by fighting. Once mature, the female can be recognized by the rounded, rather than step-like, profile of her hindquarters when viewed from the side, and she will be larger in size than the male. Never be tempted to introduce him to her quarters, because she will almost inevitably attack her intended partner. Aggression is less likely if she is placed in alongside the male, because in the wild, it is the female who journeys in search of a mate. The other alternative is to introduce the pair on neutral ground in a container with a removable partition. If the female is receptive to her intended partner, then mating will normally occur within an hour, after which the pair should be separated again.

It is usually possible to tell when the female is ready to mate by stroking her back. If she stands still with her tail raised, this is a sign that she is ready. Female hamsters come into heat

roughly every four days, so you will not have long to wait in any event. In pregnancy, the gestation period for hamsters is among the shortest of all mammals. A female Syrian hamster will produce her offspring just 16 days after mating, and the five to seven young pups will be totally helpless at birth. The normal gestation period for

Russian and Chinese hamsters will last about 19 days in both cases.

Avoid disturbing the nest as this can cause cannibalism. The young grow quickly and will start to emerge from their nest at about two weeks old. Within a further fortnight, they will be independent and should be moved to separate accommodation.

◆ RIGHT
A young Syrian hamster with its mother. Hamsters are not social by nature, and now that this youngster is feeding itself, it will need to be transferred to separate quarters to avoid fights breaking out between the pair.

GROOMING AND SHOWING

♦ BELOW
Grooming a smooth-coated hamster with a soft cloth. This can help to improve the gloss on its fur, and may also serve to remove loose hairs during the moult.

When it comes to grooming, or indeed showing, it is important that your hamster is tame and used to being handled. Hamsters have poor eyesight as, like many rodents, they spend much of their time underground in the dark. As a result, their sense of smell is significant. If you pick up a hamster too quickly, you are likely to be bitten. Instead, you need to accustom your pet to your scent. Place your hand on the floor of the cage and encourage the hamster to step on to it. You can then lift out the hamster by scooping it up, using your other hand like a cup. Avoid gripping your pet tightly, as it will then panic, struggle and bite. Occasionally, you may have to tempt your hamster into a container in order to take it out of its quarters without a struggle.

Ease of handling is another reason for starting out with a young hamster, as at this stage hamsters are far more responsive to being tamed. Taming will be virtually impossible with an older individual.

To restrain the hamster in an emergency – if it is out of its cage and is escaping under furniture, for example – hold the skin at the back of its neck. This will secure the hamster's head, so it will not be able to turn round and bite. You can then pick it up as normal to return it to its cage.

♦ LEFT
When it comes to exhibiting hamsters, not all individuals will meet the show standard. You will need some luck when breeding colour varieties with markings.

KEEPING CLEAN

Short-coated hamsters need very little grooming, although wiping them with a chamois leather, in the direction of the lie of the fur, is recommended before a show, to improve the appearance of the coat. Short-coated rexes have curly coats that do not lie flat. However, their coat care is quite straightforward as their hair is far less likely to mat. Hamsters are actually very fastidious about grooming and will usually keep themselves looking immaculate and sleek – if your pet does appear to be fluffed up with an unkempt look about it, it may indicate an illness.

Hamsters with long coats need combing once or twice a week, to prevent the hair from becoming matted and to remove bedding or pieces of food, which can get caught up here. Use a small comb with rotating teeth or a soft toothbrush. The former is a better option as it helps to break down any tangles that are forming, rather than pulling at the coat. If there is a bad knot in the coat you may have to cut it out. If you have to do this, you won't be able to show your hamster until the hair regrows to its original length.

HAMSTER SHOWS

If you are interested in showing your hamster, it is a good idea to join one of the many specialist societies, which are generally a good source of information and equipment (such as show cages).

At the show, the judges will assess the hamsters' colouring and form, and it is vital that you are aware of the show standard for the type of hamster that you are exhibiting. As well as the overall appearance or "type" of the hamster, the judges will also consider individual requirements for the different colours and coat types. Do not despair if your initial attempts at

exhibiting do not result in any wins. This is partly because hamsters are only likely to win when they are in top condition. When being judged, the condition of each entry is significant, and a hamster may win at one show and fail to be placed at the next. Always make sure you turn out your entry in immaculate condition.

♦ ABOVE
The pairing of hamsters needs to be carried out with regard to their physical appearance or type, as well as coloration, if you hope to breed exhibition winners.

♦ BELOW LEFT
Grooming a long-haired hamster is a more involved task, which needs to be carried out a couple of times a week; otherwise, the coat will become matted.

♦ BELOW
Be careful which foods you offer your hamster before a show. Avoid carrot as the juice is likely to stain the fur on the face, and this will affect the coloration, albeit temporarily.

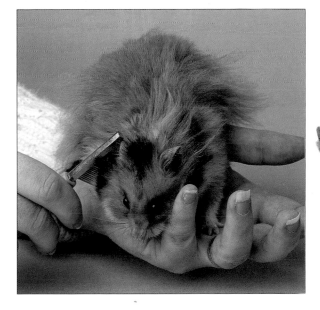

GERBILS AND JIRDS

This group of rodents is found in arid parts of the world. Like hamsters, they burrow to escape danger and the heat of the midday sun, but they are also far more agile. Their hind legs are especially well developed, and this enables them to jump long distances. In a home setting, you will need to handle them carefully to prevent them from escaping. The Mongolian gerbil has a social nature, and should be kept in pairs or trios rather than on its own.

INTRODUCTION

The Mongolian gerbil (*Meriones unguiculatus*) is the best-known member of this group – it is the most friendly of the pet gerbils – and has built up a strong following since first becoming available to pet-seekers during the 1960s. The first specimens were collected on an expedition to Mongolia by a Japanese scientist in 1954, and were bred in Japan before some stock was sent on to the United States, and then to Europe. These gerbils were actually discovered during the mid-1800s by the missionary Pere David, who travelled widely in this part of the Orient.

Mongolian gerbils are well adapted to living in desert areas, with the sandy colour of their coats and black tipping providing excellent camouflage when they are seen from above. Their underparts are white, to reflect the heat of the sand beneath them, while their long tail is also covered in fur. The tail serves as a stabilizer when the rodent is running, with its long hind legs helping to support its weight so

◆ LEFT
The natural colour of the Mongolian gerbil is called the agouti, and this helps to provide camouflage when the gerbil is viewed from above. The underparts are paler in colour.

that it can sit up and look around, jumping away if danger threatens, in a similar way to a kangaroo. Mongolian gerbils can leap 45 cm (1½ ft) to elude a would-be predator, and then quickly disappear down their burrow.

Internally, their bodies are well equipped to withstand the rigours of life in the desert. Their kidneys are incredibly efficient, allowing them

◆ LEFT
An ever-increasing range of colour mutations and varieties has been created in the case of the Mongolian gerbil, and this has led to a growing interest in exhibiting them.

to produce a very concentrated urine. This in turn means that, unlike rats and mice, gerbils have no pungent odour associated with them.

Jirds are very similar to gerbils in their habits, and the descriptions of the two species are sometimes synonymous, as in the case of the Shaw's jird which is another member of the *Meriones* genus. Like gerbils, jirds are found in arid areas. Both gerbils and jirds are found in an area ranging from North Africa through the Middle East into Asia. Only in the case of the Mongolian gerbil, however, have colour variants become widely known at present, and you may well need to track down specialist gerbil breeders in order to obtain stock of other species.

◆ BELOW
Gerbils use their long hind legs to stand up and explore their environment. You must ensure their housing is covered, to prevent any escapes.

◆ ABOVE
While balancing on its strong back legs, a gerbil may pick up and eat food using its shorter front legs, which serve rather like hands.

GERBILS AS PETS

The most important thing to bear in mind with gerbils is that they are highly social by nature, to the extent that they must be housed in groups, rather than singly. If you do not want them to breed, then you should keep them in single-sex groups. Their natural curiosity means that they are easily tamed and can be encouraged to feed quite easily from the hand.

As children's pets, gerbils have the advantage over hamsters in that they are not primarily nocturnal. Even so, they are not really pets that like to be handled or cuddled for any length of time, since they have very active natures and prefer to have the freedom to scamper about.

Although gerbils are not easy to recapture in a room because they are so agile, they are less likely to disappear in these surroundings than a hamster, for example, which may well choose to slip down under a gap in the floorboards, or disappear out of sight. Gerbils often remain on the surface and, with care and patience, it is possible to net them, or persuade them into a large cardboard box placed on its side, if food has already been placed there as a bait.

Gerbils and jirds can be expected to live for up to three years.

◆ RIGHT
When it is standing up, the gerbil relies on its tail to help to support its body. In this position, it is not just looking around but also sniffing the air, to pick up scents.

SPECIES AND BREEDS

MONGOLIAN GERBIL

A number of different colour varieties of the Mongolian gerbil have been developed. The first originated in Canada and is known as the Canadian white spot. It has a white spot on the coloured area of the body, and often has white legs and white on the tail.

A pure albino form is identified by its reddish eyes and pink ears. Up until the age of about three months or so, when the dark fur develops along the tail, it is difficult to distinguish between the albino and the dark-tailed white. At the other extreme is the pure black gerbil, known for its glossy coat. Another popular variety is the lilac, which has a bluish-grey coat (with a rosy hue) and pink eyes. Although similar, the dove grey's coat is lighter and more silvery in colour. It also has pink eyes.

A very popular variety is the predominantly gold-coloured argente, which has a white abdomen and feet, and pinkish claw and ears. The dark-eyed honey is a more unusual colour; the young, in this case, undergo a colour change at about two months old. Up until this stage, they have a yellow coat with black fur on the extremities of the body, such as the

◆ LEFT
The lilac form of the Mongolian gerbil. This colour was originally developed from crossings between the black and argente varieties. Occasional white patches do sometimes crop up on their coats.

◆ RIGHT
The argente has been described under various names, including cinnamon, golden and, perhaps most accurately, as the white-bellied golden, with a very clear delineation between white and golden areas.

◆ LEFT
The black mutation was first recorded in laboratory stock housed at the USAF School of Aerospace Medicine in Texas. Ideally, these gerbils should be pure black, with no odd white patches at all.

legs, tail and nose, giving them an appearance rather reminiscent of a Siamese cat. When they moult for the first time, these dark areas disappear from the extremities, and then ticking appears on the yellow hair of the body. As the gerbil grows older, so its white

belly patch becomes more obvious. The eyes in this case are dark, as are the nails and ears.

In the silver agouti or chinchilla form, the beige and black of the normal agouti has been modified to silvery white and black, with the belly

◆ LEFT
The Mongolian gerbil has a natural agouti coloration, with dark and light banding running down each hair, making it hard to spot from above.

◆ RIGHT
Always check on
compatibility when
considering the
purchase of other
types of gerbil or
jird. Some, such as
the relatively large
Jerusalem jird shown
here, may need to be
housed on their own.

◆ RIGHT
A pallid gerbil.
Note the relatively
large eyes, indicating
that it becomes more
active as darkness
falls. Like other
gerbils, the pallid is
very active by nature,
and jumps well, with
its tail serving as
a counterbalance.

JERUSALEM JIRD

One breed that you may occasionally encounter among the other varieties of gerbils and jirds is the Jerusalem jird (*Meriones crassus*). This variety differs significantly from its smaller Mongolian cousin in its requirements, and is very solitary by nature – to the extent that it will need to be housed on its own. The coat of the Jerusalem jird has a more reddish hue, while in terms of temperament, it tends to be less friendly than the Mongolian.

OTHER SPECIES

The attractive Egyptian gerbil (*Gerbillus gerbillus*) is sandy brown in colour. It lives on a colony basis and can become very tame. Shaw's jird (*Meriones shawi*) is found in parts of Egypt but, unfortunately, these rodents are not social by nature. Perhaps the most bizarre species of all is the fat-tailed or Duprasi's gerbil (*Pachyuromys duprasi*), which occurs in northern parts of the Sahara desert in Africa. These gerbils have a rounded body shape, and a broad, pink tail, which acts as a store for their body fat, keeping it aside to be metabolized when food rations are in short supply. The fat-tailed gerbil is nocturnal in its habits. Again, these rodents are not social by nature, and they should always be housed on their own to avoid fights.

being white. The eyes and claws are black. It has also proved possible to combine the chinchilla and dark-eyed honey mutations to create a variety known as the polar fox. This gerbil's silvery-white coloration replaces the honey coloration, although the characteristic change in markings, associated with the dark-eyed honey, is seen in this case as well. The unusual name of these gerbils stems from the similarity in appearance to the fox found in the Arctic region.

Gerbils are now being bred that display the Himalayan gene, which is responsible for the appearance of the Siamese and related cat breeds. The points of these gerbils – their legs and feet, ears, nose and tail – are dark in colour,

whereas the body is a lighter shade. Tonkinese and Burmese forms of gerbil, which show less contrast thanks to their darker overall body coloration, have also been bred; again, their names derive from breeds that exist in the cat fancy. Other new varieties of Mongolian gerbil are also being developed at present, including creams and sepia forms. These may not always be widely available.

◆ RIGHT
A number of other gerbils and jirds
are available from specialist breeders.
This is Shaw's jird, which, like its
Mongolian relative, displays a dark
tip on the upper surface of the tail.

HOUSING AND FEEDING

As gerbils are natural burrowers, it is best to house them in converted aquaria, as these allow more depth than wire-mesh cages.

GERBIL HOUSING

A lightweight acrylic tank is preferable to a glass tank because it is easier and safer to move. Equip the tank with a secure, ventilated hood to prevent the gerbils from using their jumping abilities to leap out, and to stop cats from reaching in. You should be able to acquire a special housing set-up for gerbils, which includes not only a hood but also a colour co-ordinated drinking bottle, which fits into the enclosure as part of the hood and can be removed easily from the outside.

One of the major advantages of keeping gerbils, compared with rats and mice in particular, is that they produce very little urine and so have virtually no odour associated with them. This makes caring for them more straightforward, as the lining

Gerbil mix

♦ BELOW RIGHT
Young gerbils born in a colony can be left with their parents, but you will need to check that their quarters do not become overcrowded.

♦ BELOW LEFT
Gerbils of different colours can be housed together without problems, but avoid adding newcomers to an existing colony, as this can result in fighting.

Clean out the gerbil's cage on a weekly basis, discarding the soiled shavings and replacing them with fresh ones. You will need to transfer the gerbils into a secure carrier while you clean out their quarters. A simple acrylic enclosure with a hood will suffice for this purpose, and can also serve as a suitable carrier should you need to take your gerbil to the vet. This type of carrier is much safer than a cardboard box, which gerbils will often gnaw their way out of.

in their quarters does not need to be changed as frequently. Coarse shavings, sold as small-animal bedding, should be used to line the cage. It is important not to use sawdust, as the gerbils' burrowing activities mean that their eyes can be irritated by flakes of sawdust. You can bury lengths of tubing in the substrate to allow the gerbils to explore these areas, as their own tunnels, built from shavings, could collapse. Do not forget to provide bedding material, which the gerbils can use to line their nesting chambers.

SUITABLE FOODS

Feeding gerbils is straightforward, and the procedure is the same as for other small rodents. Gerbils feed mainly on a diet of seeds, greenstuff and vegetables, and they may also eat a few invertebrates, such as mealworms. However, do not feed them large quantities of oil-based seeds, such as sunflower, as these can cause obesity, which can prove fatal. A small amount of hay is important, not just as bedding but also to add fibre to their diet. An earthenware food pot, which they will be unable to tip over, makes an ideal feeding bowl.

CONVERTED AQUARIUM SET-UP

1 It is relatively easy to set up a home for a colony of Mongolian gerbils by converting an aquarium into what is sometimes described as a gerbilarium. Ensure the tank is clean and dry before tipping in coarse wood shavings.

2 Gerbils will want to have areas where they can retreat in their enclosure, and you can help by including cardboard tubing in the substrate. Food, water and a selection of toys should also be provided.

3 A secure covering over the enclosure is important, both to stop the gerbils jumping out and to protect them from cats or dogs. A secure covering can be made using wire mesh attached to a wooden framework. Make sure the covering can be securely fixed in place.

4 As a further precaution, weigh down the roof with blocks placed at each end, which will stop any cat from being able to dislodge the lid. Note how the water bottle is suspended from the roof, allowing the gerbils to drink without difficulty.

Although gerbils do not drink large volumes of water, it is important to provide them with a supply of fresh drinking water on a daily basis. The bottle should be fixed securely in place so that it will not leak – originating from an arid area, gerbils are very susceptible to damp surroundings, and can suffer from respiratory problems.

Before you obtain a gerbil, find out what it has been feeding on, and do not change this diet for the first two weeks after rehoming. Sudden changes made during this period can lead to a fatal digestive upset. Provide your gerbil with something to gnaw to stop its teeth from overgrowing, which would prevent it from eating properly.

GENERAL CARE AND BREEDING

◆ BELOW
Gerbils can be quite tame, but when moving
your pet out of its quarters, restraining it by
the base of the tail will prevent any escapes.

Gerbils are surprisingly agile creatures, able to escape encircling fingers by using their powerful hind legs to jump out of your grasp. They are not pets that enjoy being handled, although they will often feed from the hand.

HANDLING
When you need to restrain a gerbil, start by allowing it to sniff at your fingers, and then gently coax it on to your hand. Place your other hand on top, so that the gerbil can see out but will still feel reasonably secure. Since it is not being held tightly, it will also be unlikely to bite under these circumstances.

Handling a gerbil can sometimes be rather alarming because, acting on instinct, it will often faint in the same way that it would if caught by a predator. Some strains of gerbils are more prone to this behaviour than others. If a gerbil does react in this way, the best thing to do is to place it in a quiet spot and it will soon recover.

Although you can restrain a gerbil by gently holding the base of its tail close to the body, never grasp it by the tip of its tail. The skin here is very loose and sheds rapidly, resulting in bleeding and even partial loss of the tail. Again, this is a defensive mechanism that helps the gerbil to escape from a predator. Careful handling should prevent this from being a problem.

MATING AND PREGNANCY
It is important to sex gerbils correctly at the outset as they will need to be kept in single-sex groups; if not, you will almost certainly end up with unexpected litters. Male gerbils can be identified easily by comparing the length of their ano-genital gap with that of the females, since this space is significantly longer. Once mature, male gerbils are also significantly larger than females and are nearly twice as heavy.

When breeding Mongolian gerbils, introduce the male and female carefully. Initially, place them both in neutral territory. Some acrylic containers have a divider, so, after a couple of days, the two gerbils can be allowed direct contact by removing the partition. Even so, watch for any signs of aggression, although normally there are no problems under these circumstances, and mating soon takes place. The pair should be left together for about a week, after which they can be separated.

◆ LEFT
Sexing gerbils is straightforward, with the male shown on the left here. The swellings caused by the testicles will be less evident in younger males.

◆ RIGHT
When picking up a gerbil, do not hold it tightly in your hand but cup it gently, as shown here.

✦ BELOW
The long tail of the gerbil acts as a
counterbalance, helping to ensure that
when the gerbil jumps, using its powerful
limbs, it will usually land safely.

✦ BOTTOM
Young Mongolian gerbils can remain within an
established colony, provided that the group will
not be overcrowded.

It is not a good idea to leave
the male with the female because she
can mate again very soon after giving
birth, and this will mean that the
gerbils are likely to produce an
unexpected second litter. About
24 days after mating, a female will
typically give birth to five cubs,
which are without fur and totally
helpless at this early stage, usually
measuring about 2.5 cm (1 in) in
length. The young gerbils will grow
rapidly, and can be weaned once they
are about five or six weeks of age.
They are likely to be mature after
a similar period of time, and will
continue to breed well until the age
of about 14 months old.

✦ LEFT
Young gerbils can
be weaned at five
or six weeks. They
will be mature about
6 weeks later, and
will breed well up
to 14 months.

GROOMING AND SHOWING

◆ BELOW
Gerbils being judged at a show. It is important
that exhibition gerbils are used to being
handled from an early age, so that they are not
frightened by this experience.

Gerbils need very little grooming
in order to look immaculate, partly
because no long-coated mutation has
yet been developed, and their coats
are not prone to becoming tangled.
In addition, gerbils frequently clean
themselves. However, for exhibition
purposes, a degree of tidying-up will
usually be necessary to ensure that
your gerbils are looking their best.

SHOW PREPARATION

The most common problem is that the
coat may have become stained by juice
from greenstuff, particularly the area
around the face. It is a good idea to
leave items such as carrot and cabbage
out of the gerbil's diet for a week
beforehand as it may be difficult to
remove these stains, especially as it is
not advisable to wash the coat. Aside

from the stress involved, there is a risk
that the gerbil could develop a chill.
Serious exhibitors often resort to
using corn flour to mask stained areas,
carefully moistening the area and
rubbing in the corn flour. Once it has
dried, the area needs to be brushed
very gently to remove all trace of the
powder. If you place the gerbil in a
hay-lined box, it will burrow in and

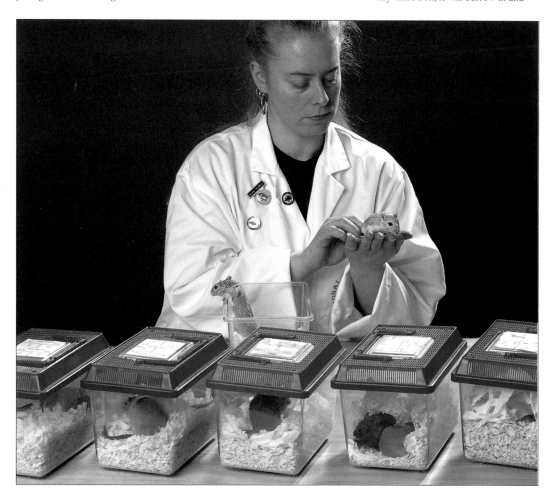

◆ BELOW
Condition is very important in exhibition gerbils. Beware of offering too much sunflower seed as this is fattening, and may even shorten the gerbil's lifespan.

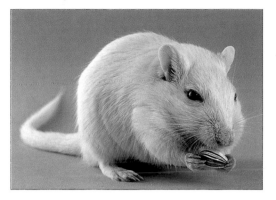

◆ RIGHT
Gerbils are shown individually, so you will have to wait until a female has given birth and her litter are independent before showing her again.

◆ BOTTOM
You will need to be familiar with the show standard for particular varieties, in terms of coloration and patterning.

◆ BELOW
Always ensure that your gerbil is in perfect condition prior to entering a show. Any loss of hair or damage to the tip of the tail will almost always count against it.

this will have the effect of grooming the coat. Finally, stroking the gerbil with a silk cloth helps to impart a good gloss to its fur.

GERBIL SHOWS
Standard show cages for gerbils are essential for serious exhibitors. For pet classes, however, the gerbils' regular home can be used, although you should cut down on the bedding for the show, so that the judge will be able to see your entry easily. It is also very important that the judge will be able to handle your gerbil without difficulty. If you hope to show your pet gerbil, you will need to train it when it is young to get it used to handling. In addition to the condition of the gerbil and its tameness, the judges will also look at its surroundings. An otherwise excellent entry will be penalized if exhibited in a dirty or chipped show cage. It is important to maintain show cages or pens in top condition by washing them out after each show. After they have dried, keep them dust free by storing them in plastic bags until required again.

One of the aspects of showing is its unpredictability. There is no guarantee that just because one gerbil won at its last show that it will do so again at the next event. The gerbil could be moulting, for example, so that its coat is not in top condition. As with other small livestock, the gerbils in a show class are not judged against each other, but rather against an ideal for the particular variety concerned. After the judging has taken place, most judges will be happy to offer advice concerning your gerbils.

RATS AND MICE

While these rodents may not top the list of everyone's favourite pet, they can turn out to be truly excellent companions, with rats in particular proving to be highly intelligent. Although rats and mice are very similar in appearance, rats are distinguished by their larger size. They must not be housed together, since rats will often instinctively attack mice. The choice of colours available in the case of rats is far less varied than it is with mice.

INTRODUCTION

Although rats and mice have a justified reputation for spreading various unpleasant diseases, the simple fact is that today's domesticated, or "fancy", rats and mice are far removed from their wild relatives, and are unlikely to present any significant health risks to people keeping them.

The process of domestication began well over a century ago, when rats were a major cause of disease in densely populated cities. The high death toll from rat-induced infections led to the employment of rat-catchers to keep a check on their numbers.

On occasion, the rat-catchers would catch rats that were different in colour to the normal type. These oddities were often kept on display at public houses, whereas their less fortunate relatives were killed by dogs in rat pits for customer entertainment.

✦ ABOVE
The brown rat is the original ancestor of all of today's fancy rats, although the black rat was also kept and bred for a period.

✦ LEFT
The wild form of the house mouse, with its typical brownish coloration – far removed from today's colourful domesticated mouse varieties.

By this stage in history, the brown rat (*Rattus norvegicus*) had become far more numerous than the black rat (*Rattus rattus*), and all of today's fancy rats are of brown rat descent, although different-coloured strains of black rat were kept during the 1920s.

The keeping of fancy rats lost favour for a period after this era until the 1970s. Since then, however, there has been much interest in keeping these intelligent rodents as pets and for exhibition purposes, and more colour varieties have been established.

RATS AND MICE AS PETS

When it comes to choosing between a mouse or a rat as a pet, it is worth bearing in mind that rats are significantly larger, averaging at least 25 cm (10 in) in length, and will consequently need more spacious accommodation. Mice typically measure around 15 cm (6 in) overall, including their tail. Rats have a significantly longer lifespan than mice, living on average for five years or more, while mice have a lifespan of around three years. Rats are also more likely to become tamer and are more amenable to handling. The strong odour of both rats and mice can be a

problem in the home environment, although females tend to produce a less pungent urine than males and may make a more suitable pet. While rats are typically kept on their own, mice can be housed comfortably in single-sex pairs or even trios.

It is important to buy pet mice and rats when they are young so that they accept being handled. They are then far less likely to inflict a painful bite when picked up.

Rats and mice are nocturnal by instinct, but they will usually be active during the day as well. Ensure that the fur looks sleek when you buy – if it is not, it could be a sign of ill-health, particularly if the rodent also appears to be hunched up.

The domestication of the fancy mouse from its wild ancestor, the house mouse (*Mus musculus*), first began in the United Kingdom in the latter part of the 19th century. As in the case of rats, mice were widely used for medical experiments at this time,

although their show potential was quickly recognized. The National Mouse Club in the United Kingdom was established in 1895 and is the oldest body of its kind in the world. Its creation led to the development of a vast colour range of fancy mice.

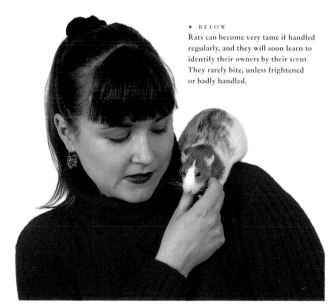

COLOUR VARIETIES

While there are now over 700 different varieties of mice, the number of fancy rat mutations is much lower, totalling less than 30. In most cases, the choice of colours available in most pet stores is small, so if you are seeking out some of the more unusual colours, you will usually need to contact a breeder. Look through the advertisement columns of specialist magazines or contact clubs. Details can usually be obtained through local libraries or via the Internet.

RATS

Breeds of rat that are furthest removed from the natural agouti form are the most popular. The most widely kept variety of rat is the albino form, sometimes called the white, which is distinguished by its pink eyes. Its lack of colour pigment also accounts for its pink ears and tail. Most of the new rat varieties have direct counterparts in

◆ ABOVE
The silvered mink is just one of a growing number of exotic colour varieties of the domestic rat. All are descended from the brown rather than the black rat.

◆ BELOW
A Himalayan rat, so-called because of the darker areas of fur present on the extremities of the body. These will be far less apparent in newly born pups.

◆ ABOVE
An agouti and white rat. The agouti colouring corresponds to that of the wild brown rat, which explains why these varieties are not the most popular choice as domestic pets.

◆ LEFT
A silvered black rat. At shows, it is not just the coloration of these rodents that is judged, but also their physical appearance, or "type".

the mouse fancy, with the exception of the mink. This rat is coffee coloured, with a bluish sheen to its coat.

Darker colours include the chocolate, which should be an even dark shade, as well as the black, which must also be pure in colour with no odd white hairs visible in its coat. In addition, there are other self (solid colour) varieties with pink eyes and a rosy hue – including the champagne, which is beige. The patterned colour variants include the hooded, which has a coloured area over its head and shoulders, extending down the back to the base of the tail. In the case of the capped form, there is no darker streak running back down the spine, and the remainder of the fur is white. There is no long-coated form, although there is a rex mutation, which has distinctive curled fur and whiskers.

The features of the long-coated and
rex variants can be combined with any
colour form or patterning. The scope
here is truly enormous, and some
fascinating specimens can be seen at
the larger mice shows.

♦ BELOW
Even coloration is an important feature of
the silver-grey variety. Sometimes, the body
extremities may lack adequate silvering. This
individual is a buck (male).

MICE

There are both self and patterned
varieties of fancy mice. One of the
most striking is the self red, which is
a rich shade of chestnut. Its coloration
is improved by the addition of a satin
mutation, which gives a glossy sheen
to the coat. The eyes are black, but
some varieties, such as white and
cream, exist in both pink-eyed and
black-eyed forms. Evenness
of colour through the coat
is an essential attribute
for self-coloured mice of
all varieties.

Tan varieties are instantly
recognizable by their appearance.
Their underparts are tan-coloured,
while the remainder of the body is
a contrasting shade. The feet should
match the body colour on the outside
and be tan-coloured on the inside.
Nor is it just dark shades such
as black and tan that
are regularly seen.
Lighter variants,
too, such as silver
and tan, are quite
commonly bred.
    Mice showing
various other markings are
also widely kept today.
These include Himalayans,
with dark points, and
the Dutch, which has
a similar pattern
to that of the
corresponding guinea
pig or rabbit breeds.

♦ ABOVE
The chinchilla mouse is so-called because it
resembles the wild chinchilla in colour. The
individual hairs are tipped with black, and
the undercoat is slate blue.

♦ BELOW
The black form of the mouse must be jet
black, with a glossy coat. Mice of this colour
were first recorded as far back as 1640. Any
white markings are a serious flaw.

♦ ABOVE
A black and tan
mouse. The tan
underparts are most
obvious when these
mice sit up on
their haunches.
There must be clear
delineation between
the colours, as in
this individual.

HOUSING AND FEEDING

Caring for rats and mice in the home does not present problems, providing the housing is roomy and secure and the diet is suitably nutritious.

ACCOMMODATION

The range of housing options for rats and mice has grown significantly over recent years. Special cages are now available that provide plenty of climbing space and are essentially escape proof – a highly important consideration when keeping these rodents in the home as, once free, they can be difficult to recapture. To be extra safe, it is worthwhile adding a small combination lock to the door.

If you prefer not to use a mesh cage – which can be a magnet to a cat – an acrylic container with a ventilated roof is a suitable alternative. This lightweight option is easy to move around but, as with any housing for pets in the home, be sure not to position the cage resting on furniture in front of a window. In hot weather, your pet may be affected by heat stress, with the glass magnifying the

sun's rays. Rats and mice are also nocturnal creatures and bright daylight can upset their sleep patterns. Position cages in a draught-free place because, in spite of the hardiness of their wild relatives, domestic rats and mice are susceptible to chilling.

♦ ABOVE
A cage for rats. Take care to ensure the rodents are not overcrowded. Otherwise, not only disease but fighting, too, can break out.

♦ LEFT
Toys of various types appeal to the inquisitive nature of rats and mice. If you provide a wheel, it must be of an enclosed design to prevent tail injuries.

♦ RIGHT
Paper bedding is one hygienic option and is readily obtainable from pet stores. It is less likely to trigger respiratory problems, being relatively free from dust.

Most cages for rats are equipped with a detachable metal tray where the droppings collect. It is a good idea to line the tray with shavings but do not use this as a lining material in the rats' quarters, where they can burrow directly into it. A better option for this purpose is to use dust-free bedding also sold in pet stores.

Both mice and rats are shy creatures so it is essential to provide them with a thick layer of bedding in a corner of their quarters where they can retreat

Rat mix

Sunflower seeds

Peanuts

Dog biscuits

and curl up to sleep. A wooden box surrounding this area will give them greater security. Special paper bedding is a better option than hay as both rats and mice are susceptible to respiratory diseases, and these can be triggered by the dust and fungal spores in hay.

SUITABLE FOODS
You can feed your rodent a seed-based diet, which contains cereals such as wheat and flaked maize (corn), or, preferably, a pelleted diet, which contains all the necessary ingredients to keep rats and mice in good health.

◆ ABOVE, BELOW LEFT AND BELOW RIGHT
Retreats are very important, allowing rats and mice to feel secure in their quarters; the natural instinct of small mammals is to stay hidden, out of sight of possible predators.

If you are not feeding your rodent a pre-formulated diet you may need to use a supplement to compensate for any nutritional deficiencies. Sprinkle the supplement over the rodent's favourite tidbits. When it comes to fresh food, it is best to offer it in small amounts on a regular basis. Although it will not contribute greatly to the protein intake, it will provide valuable vitamins and minerals. Large amounts of fresh food eaten at one time can trigger digestive upsets.

Avoid using mixes that contain significant proportions of oil seeds, such as sunflower or peanuts. These are not recommended for rats and mice on a long-term basis as they are likely to provoke skin irritations. There is no harm in offering other treats occasionally, such as small cubes of cheddar cheese and raisins.

The occasional sunflower seed or nut can be used when taming your rodent to feed from the hand. Otherwise, attempts to hand-feed could lead to bitten fingers.

A water bottle that attaches to the rodent's quarters and an earthenware food container are both essential.

GENERAL CARE AND BREEDING

You can purchase accessories of various kinds for the enclosure, but bear in mind that mice and especially rats can inflict damage on plastic items, and these may need to be replaced in due course. It is actually much better to provide them with wooden blocks for chewing purposes or dried crusts of bread, on which they can wear down their incisor teeth. Avoid exercise wheels which have an open-weave design, as the rodent's long tail may become trapped.

Some household items can also be used to amuse your rodent, such as the lining tubes out of paper towelling, which make excellent tunnels. Rats are very playful by nature, and glass marbles that can be rolled along with their paws are another item that often appeals to them; glass marbles will also prove indestructible.

HANDLING

The handling of rodents requires particular care, as rats and mice have poor eyesight and rely more on their

sense of smell for information about the world around them. If you attempt to pick one up too suddenly, you are likely to be bitten. Instead, allow the rodent to sniff at your fingers, and then gently scoop it up from beneath. Your new pet will quickly come to recognize your distinctive scent and

will become much more amenable to regular handling. Even so, take care not to clench your pet tightly – this will make it panic and it could then bite – but allow it to rest in your hand. If necessary, mice can be restrained from scampering off by gently grasping the base of their tails.

◆ ABOVE
Handling a mouse. Do not try to grip your pet tightly in order to restrain it. Instead, encourage the rodent to step on to your hand and hold it gently by the base of the tail.

◆ LEFT
Rats are slightly more difficult to hold than mice because of their larger size, but they will rest in the hand for short periods, being cupped in this way, without attempting to bite or struggle.

◆ ABOVE
Rats will step readily from one hand to another, usually sniffing cautiously before they do so. Many will also perch on your shoulder.

NEWBORN RATS

Young rats are helpless and blind at birth. Do not disturb them at this stage because it could cause the doe to abandon them. Dark markings indicate black fur.

One of the features of rodents is the speed at which their young develop. This litter of rat pups is 12 days old and their coloration is already apparent. They sleep together for warmth.

A three weeks old, these young rats are moving and exploring their environment. It will be a further two weeks, however, before they are fully weaned and able to go to a new home.

♦ RIGHT
The rapid growth of young rodents can be seen by comparing the size of the younger four-week-old rat here with its larger companion, which is just a fortnight older.

MATING AND PREGNANCY

This is a relatively straightforward procedure. Male rats and mice, known as bucks, have the typical longer ano-genital gap and a visible scrotal sac. Females (does) in general are smaller in size. If you want to encourage mating, introduce the pair to neutral territory and leave them together for up to a fortnight, by which time mating will have taken place. The doe should then be housed on her own in preparation for the birth. Pregnancy lasts about 23 days in the case of rats, and a couple of days less in the case of mice. Rats may have slightly larger litters on average, comprising ten or more pups, which can be separated from their mother at five to six weeks old. Young mice pups should be weaned at three weeks old. Mice will often reach maturity at three months of age.

NEWBORN MICE

The breeding cycle of mice is faster than that of rats, but otherwise similar. No special foods are required for rearing purposes.

Young mice aged ten days old with their mother. The pup on the far right is smaller than its nest mates and is the runt of the litter.

Mice at 25 days, which have been weaned. The genetics surrounding the breeding of different colours have been intensively studied.

GROOMING AND SHOWING

Coat care for rodents is generally minimal, although long-coated mice do require grooming to prevent the hair becoming matted or soiled by bedding underneath. Exhibitors often have their own particular ways of conditioning their stock prior to a major show but, in many cases, it is possible simply to take rats or mice from their regular cages, transfer them to show cages and go on to win without any further preparation.

SHOW PREPARATION

To improve the sheen on your pet's coat, gently groom it with a piece of silk in the direction of the lie. As condition is very important in the judging process, do not expect your rodent to win if it is moulting. There is nothing that can be done here other than allowing the new fur to grow. It is worth noting, too, that a mouse or rat that is out of condition could be vulnerable to illness.

✦ ABOVE
Rats need little in the way of grooming, and keeping the fur free of food or bedding material is usually the most that will be required.

✦ BELOW
The condition of the mice is very important for show purposes, and those that are moulting are unlikely to excel. The Maxey show cage is typically used for exhibiting mice.

AT THE SHOW

It is well worth visiting shows, even if you are not entering any rats or mice yourself. This will give you the opportunity to study the entries and build up an image in your mind's eye of the ideal for your particular variety.

To gain even greater insight into the exhibition side of the hobby, you could volunteer to steward at show events. Stewarding itself entails taking the entries and facilitating the judging process by removing the hay, for example, from the Maxey show cages, allowing the judge to remove the mice more easily so that they can be examined individually. As a steward, you will be able to see how judges assess the entries at close quarters, and, after judging has occurred, you can ask the judge about the points that have influenced the placings.

Judging standards are laid down for the different varieties. These relate firstly to the overall appearance of the rats and mice in general terms, specifying what is considered to be desirable, such as the shape of the head

A wide variety of different retreats can be purchased for mice, although plastic designs are preferable to wood, because they will not become stained by urine.

It is not a good idea to allow your pet mouse to exercise in the garden, as these rodents are very nimble and can quickly run off and disappear from view.

and ears. They also highlight serious flaws, such as kinked tails, which would merit penalties – including possible disqualification – although it is unlikely that rodents with these weaknesses would have been entered in the first place.

Then there are the more specific requirements – depending on the variety concerned – that specify the pattern of markings or the desired depth of coloration. Condition is not overlooked either, with obese entries being penalized, while ease of handling is another important factor that can help to influence a judge's decision. Those varieties that are not yet standardized because there are too few examples in existence, are usually grouped together. Assuming that the popularity of these varieties continues to grow among fanciers, and no major weaknesses crop up in the bloodlines, then these are likely to be recognized with specific official standards in due course and will be transferred into classes of their own.

Red-eyed white mice are popular pets. This may be linked to the fact that they appear very clean, thanks to the colour of their fur.

CHINCHILLAS

The requirements of these rodents are rather different from other members of the group. Chinchillas are also more costly to purchase, although this is balanced to some extent by their relatively long lifespan. As quite new entrants on the show scene, chinchillas are not widely exhibited as yet. However, there are signs that this state of affairs is changing, particularly as new colour varieties are becoming more commonly available.

INTRODUCTION

Chinchillas belong to the caviomorph sub-group in the rodent family and, as such, are closely related to guinea pigs. Like guinea pigs, chinchillas originate from the Andean region of South America, on the western side of this continent, and are found at relatively high altitudes where the temperature can become very cold, particularly at night. They are well equipped to survive in this type of terrain, however, thanks to their very dense coat. In fact, the coat is so dense (there can be 70 or more hairs growing from a single hair follicle) that parasites cannot become established in it.

Unfortunately, this very dense, soft fur proved ideal for clothing and accessories, and this led to the Spanish explorers of South America taking

✦ LEFT
The mountain viscacha, which lives in the Andean region of South America, is closely related to the chinchilla. It has similarly dense fur but much larger ears.

✦ BELOW LEFT
A young viscacha in the wild. All members of the family Chinchillidae produce fewer offspring than other rodents and after a longer gestation period.

chinchillas back to Europe in the early 1500s. The growing European and North American demand during the 1800s led to the determined hunting of these rodents for the fur trade. By the early 1900s the chinchilla was becoming an endangered species.

The first efforts to farm chinchillas for their fur proved unsuccessful, and by the time a mining engineer called M. F. Chapman tried to obtain chinchillas for a further attempt, during the 1920s, they were on the verge of extinction. It took 23 men three years to obtain just 11 live examples for him. Fortunately, this was sufficient to establish the first chinchilla fur farm and, also, ultimately, to safeguard the future of these unique rodents.

After careful acclimatization from the Andean mountains to sea level, the chinchillas were taken by ship to California, where they started

♦ RIGHT
The soft, dense coat
of the chinchilla
proved so popular
with furriers that
it nearly brought
about the extinction
of the species.

♦ BELOW
The coloration of
both the chinchilla
and the mountain
viscacha, seen here,
help them to blend
into the background
in the wild.

breeding rapidly. Stock initially changed hands at high prices, but by the 1960s the appeal of chinchillas started to grow. They started to be sold as pets for the first time, and the market for their fur began to decline.

CHINCHILLAS AS PETS

Chinchillas are now highly popular around the world as companion animals. They are still more expensive than other pet rodents but their exclusivity and clean image has helped them to become favourite pets. As chinchillas tend to be more active at dusk, they are a good choice of companion for people who are out at work all day, and they can become very tame, especially if handled regularly from an early age. Unlike the guinea pig, the chinchilla is very much a household pet and it will require special care and grooming. Chinchillas have sharp incisor teeth, which can inflict serious damage on plastic food containers and play equipment in their cages; these will need to be checked and replaced on a regular basis.

Unlike many rodents, chinchillas have an unusually long lifespan, and can live for over a decade. Some have been known to live for over 20 years.

COLOUR VARIETIES

◆ BELOW
The charcoal variant of the chinchilla, which is of a darker shade than the standard. Although more expensive than the usual form, their care needs are identical.

The typical wild form of the chinchilla, known as the standard, is variable in colour, with light and dark bands encircling the individual hairs, creating a slightly mottled impression over the body. The depth of colouring differs between individuals, ranging from shades of grey through to black, with the hairs darkest at the tips. In contrast, the fur on the underside of the body is pure white. The eyes are always black and the ears, too, are dark in colour.

WHITE FORMS

The palest varieties now available are the white forms. The true white is pure white in colour, sometimes displaying odd darker patches. It is not a true albino, as it may have some black hairs on the body and has black ears and eyes. This is in contrast to the

◆ BELOW
The alert nature of the chinchilla is clearly displayed by this standard individual, with its large ears helping to pinpoint the direction of sounds with great accuracy.

pink white where the presence of any pigment is restricted to traces of beige colouring. The ears and paws are both pink, and the eyes may vary in colour from pink to red, emphasizing the lack of dark melanin pigment in the white chinchilla form.

BEIGE FORMS

There are two forms of beige chinchillas, and these differ in their genetic make-up and thus, their coloration. The pure homozygous beige is paler in colour than its heterozygous counterpart, and is a very pale shade of cream with a slight pink suffusion. The eyes in this case are also a pale shade of pink, with a whitish ring surrounding the pupil at the centre of each eye. Heterozygous beige chinchillas vary in colour from cream through to shades of dark beige, with significantly paler underparts, as in the standard variety. The eye coloration of the heterozygous is often more clearly defined, ranging from pink through to red.

◆ BELOW
A young standard chinchilla. As with related members of the caviomorph group of rodents, including the guinea pig, they are born in an advanced state of development.

◆ BELOW
The standard varies in its depth of coloration. This is a dark individual, but note that the whiter underparts are retained. Fresh tidbits can be offered regularly to these rodents.

BROWN EBONY FORMS

The brown ebony can be distinguished by its even brown fur over its body, and contrasting pink ears and eyes. The ebony is entirely black in colour, while the charcoal mutation is grey, including the underparts and the paws.

VIOLET FORMS

One of the more recent varieties to capture the imagination of chinchilla breeders is the violet. Here, the body colour is a softer shade of grey, and it is distinguished from the charcoal chinchilla form by white underparts. As with some of the other recent colour varieties, the violet form will doubtless become more widely available as its popularity grows.

COLOUR BREEDING

Chinchilla breeding, as far as colours is concerned, is still rather a hobby in its infancy, and it offers plenty of scope for the future. Not all pairing can be carried out safely for genetic reasons. White chinchillas, for example, must

not be paired together. Outcrossing, as this is known, is also recommended for the black velvet mutation, where the depth of colour can vary from a matt shade of black on the body to a more glossy colour across the back.

◆ RIGHT
The fawn mutation of the chinchilla is markedly different in terms of coloration, compared with the usual form, with its coat displaying a decidedly brownish tone.

The underparts are much paler than the body in this case. Brown velvets can be distinguished from their black counterparts by their coloration, but again, these chinchillas should not be paired together for breeding purposes.

HOUSING AND FEEDING

◆ BELOW
A typical chinchilla cage. All-mesh designs are generally used for these rodents. They should be given quite spacious surroundings in view of their size and active natures.

Chinchillas require spacious indoor quarters, and it is now easy to find cages for them from pet suppliers. It is also possible to convert sectional cat pens into suitable accommodation, bearing in mind that chinchillas like to spend time off the ground.

CAGE DESIGN

A pair of chinchillas can be housed in a cage measuring about 50 cm (20 in) square by approximately 1 m (1 yd) high. The mesh spacing should not exceed 5 x 2.5 cm (2 x 1 in) in the case of adult chinchillas, and half this size for young animals. If you are making an enclosure yourself, it is important to use mesh which is at least 16 gauge or thicker, to resist their sharp teeth. All timber should be placed on the outside of the cage for this reason.

◆ BELOW
Providing a floor covering on the tray of the chinchilla cage. Shavings are ideal for this purpose but, as always, only use those sold as animal bedding.

A metal base, on which the enclosure can stand, is a much more durable option than a plastic tray, which your pet could destroy, but it is important to ensure that there are no sharp edges where the chinchillas might cut themselves. They need to be provided with thick branches to climb up and gnaw. These should not be cut from trees that have recently been sprayed with chemicals, or which might prove to be poisonous, such as yew, laburnum or fresh pine. Sycamore or manzanita are good choices; they provide straight wood and are resistant to the chinchillas' teeth. Branches from apple trees are another hard-wearing alternative, and these are quite commonly available.

Ensure that these lengths of wood are held securely in place, however, because if they do fall down they could seriously or even fatally injure the occupants. Large netting staples, fixed across the mesh from outside the cage, will serve to hold the branches in place; take care to ensure they do not become exposed as the timber is gnawed away. It is also a good idea to include a nest box for the chinchillas, where they can sleep. It should measure 50 cm (20 in) in length and 25 cm (10 in) in width and height, and should be placed

Hay

Shavings

Log

Pellets

Water
bottle

Dust bath

Nest box
lined with hay

on the floor. There should also be a
climbing shelf where they can rest,
but this must be made of mesh that is
no larger than 1 cm (½ in) square, to
protect the rodent's legs and feet from
any injury.

To wear their teeth down, a special
pumice block should be provided in
the quarters. Never offer them
ordinary rodent foods containing
seeds, and restrict treats to a small
piece of fresh-cut apple or a couple of

raisins each day. Fresh drinking water
should be provided in a drinking
bottle attached to the outside of the
cage; provide a metal screen to protect
the water bottle from the risk of being
punctured by sharp chinchilla teeth.

CHINCHILLA FOODS

As the dietary needs of chinchillas
are highly specific, you need to feed
them with special chinchilla pellets
which may have to be bought by mail
order. Even a change of brand needs
to be carried out gradually, over a few
weeks, to avoid the risk of diarrhoea,
which may prove to be fatal. On
average, an adult chinchilla will eat
about 35 g (1¼ oz) of pellets each day.
Special feeders that dispense pellets
from outside the cage will prevent
any soiling of the food.

Chinchillas are adapted to a high
fibre diet, and the only other food
required to meet their nutritional
needs is a constant supply of good
quality meadow hay. Alfalfa cubes are
an alternative to increase the fibre in
the diet and can be provided alongside
a reduced quantity of hay.

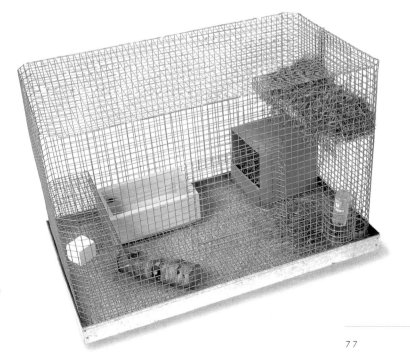

GENERAL CARE AND GROOMING

◆ LEFT
In spite of their active natures, chinchillas can be handled quite easily, especially if picked up regularly from an early age. Adequate support stops them struggling.

Handling chinchillas is not difficult, especially when they are tame. Simply encircle the body with your hand and lift up the chinchilla, providing adequate support for its underparts. Restrain a less friendly animal by holding the base of the tail gently and using your other hand to pick it up.

SAFETY IN THE HOME

Chinchillas appreciate exercise outside their cage but you must adapt your room to ensure your pet's safety. Check that there are no trailing electrical cables leading up to power sockets, which could be gnawed, and move valuable furniture out of reach. Never leave your chinchilla alone in a room as it might start chewing on wooden furniture and may ingest harmful paints or wood preservatives.

Most chinchillas develop a routine when they are out of their quarters and will return to their cages by themselves in due course. While free they may soil the room, although they can be trained to use a litter tray. Chinchillas are clean animals, with no unpleasant odour, but the cage will need to be cleaned out once a week. Keep the chinchillas away from their floor covering as much as possible – it can be harmful if ingested – and do not allow them to gnaw on cedarwood or cardboard. Since chinchillas will usually soil the same part of their cage, it is a good idea to add baking soda to the lining on the floor here, which will serve as a non-toxic deodorizer.

COAT CARE

The unique coat of a chinchilla needs attention to maintain condition. This is achieved with regular dust baths.

Using a formulated dusting powder made from volcanic ash or activated clay (other materials can be harmful), pour a layer of 5 cm (2 in) in a shallow box or on a tray. Place this on the floor of the cage. By rolling about in the dust, the chinchilla will remove excess grease from its coat. After five minutes the bath can be removed. Chinchillas require a dust bath two or three times a week, although heavily pregnant chinchillas should not dust bathe until their kits are about a week old. You can also comb their distinctive coats using a chinchilla comb: the hair will stand upright away from the body.

Damage and hair loss do occur on occasion, with fur nibbling often being a sign of stress. It may be that the chinchilla does not feel secure in its quarters, possibly because it does not have a nest box for sleeping purposes. Overcrowding can also lead to fur damage – an affected individual may be being bullied. Hair loss around the nipples is normal in the case of females that are suckling offspring; this will regrow once her kits are weaned.

◆ LEFT
Preparing a dust bath. This is an essential part of the chinchilla grooming process.

◆ RIGHT
A dust bath helps to keep the coat free from grease. It should only be offered for a few minutes, and should be withheld from pregnant females who are about to give birth.

BREEDING AND SHOWING

Although they mature between three and five months of age, it is not recommended to breed from chinchillas for the first time until they reach seven months old.

MATING AND PREGNANCY

Female chinchillas have a shorter gap between their anal and genital openings than males, and are smaller in size when adult. The female has a relatively long breeding cycle and only comes into heat once a month. Pairings need to be made carefully to avoid genetic incompatibility and to minimize any risk of fighting when the pair are introduced. Place them in adjoining cages and then, after a few days, if they are showing an interest in each other, transfer the male into the female's quarters. Assuming all goes well, he can be left in there with her until after the young are born and are independent.

◆ ABOVE LEFT AND ABOVE RIGHT
The sexing of chinchillas is done by examining their underparts. The female is seen here on the right. Note the swelling of the male's scrotal sac.

◆ LEFT
A fawn chinchilla baby at two days of age with its mother. The difference in size is very obvious, and it will be at least six weeks before the youngster is independent.

◆ BELOW LEFT
A young chinchilla. Note the relatively short tail, and the covering of short fur here. It has a long potential lifespan, often living for ten years or more.

only cause of this. Pregnancy lasts for 16 weeks. Three young will be born in an advanced state of development, as miniature adults, with their eyes open. At this stage, they weigh up to 55 g (2 oz), less than a tenth of the weight of an adult. The young chinchillas, known as kits, will be suckled by their mother for six to eight weeks before they are fully independent.

EXHIBITIONS

Chinchillas are not commonly exhibited at present but as the number of colour varieties

◆ BELOW
An older fawn chinchilla. The coat by this stage is much more developed, and the brush of longer fur on the tail is clearly apparent, compared with the youngster.

One of the most reliable signs of pregnancy is the presence of a white plug of mucus, called a stopper, on the floor of the cage. This is produced by the female. She may also adopt an unusual sleeping posture, although the impending arrival of a litter is not the

continues to increase this situation is changing. Chinchillas may be seen at larger small-animal shows, as well as at events organized by chinchilla clubs. Standardization of the chinchilla's type is underway because of pressure on coat quality, following selective breeding for fur over the generations.

When travelling with chinchillas it is vital to remember that they are highly susceptible to heat stroke in temperatures above 25°C (77°F). This applies even in the home, where they may need to be transferred to a cooler location on particularly hot days.

OTHER SMALL MAMMALS

Several other different types of rodents and other small mammals are becoming popular with enthusiasts, although their requirements tend to be more specialist than in the case of the more regular pet rodents. These mammals make original and charming pets, but they can be expensive to buy and you will often need to spend more time tracking down appropriate food and equipment suppliers.

SPECIALITY PETS

Always aim to find out as much as you can about the needs of your pet before you take it home. The breeder from whom you buy the animal will be able to advise on most aspects of its care.

CHIMPUNK

One of the most widely kept members of this group is the Siberian chipmunk (*Eutamias sibiricus*). This is an attractive shade of brown with darker stripes running down its back and white underparts. These rodents measure about 10 cm (4 in) long, with a slightly shorter tail. They can be housed either indoors or out, in an aviary-like structure. Provide plenty of branches for climbing purposes.

The wooden supports of the cage should be built on the outside, out of reach of the chipmunk's strong teeth. The mesh for the frames should be 16 gauge in thickness, with a strand size no bigger than 2.5 x 1 cm (1 x ½ in). The base must be solid to prevent escapes and to ensure that other rodents cannot tunnel their way in.

+ RIGHT
A Korean chipmunk housed in a large indoor bird cage. These rodents are very lively and agile by nature. Note the nest box provided as a retreat, and the wooden branch for climbing purposes – this may also be gnawed on occasion.

+ BELOW LEFT
The spikey appearance of the fur is one of the characteristic features of spiny mice. These rodents need to be handled with particular care, since their tails are easily injured.

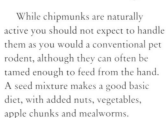

While chipmunks are naturally active you should not expect to handle them as you would a conventional pet rodent, although they can often be tamed enough to feed from the hand. A seed mixture makes a good basic diet, with added nuts, vegetables, apple chunks and mealworms.

Provide a nest box for roosting and breeding. Between four and eight young will be born after a gestation period of 31 days. The young leave the nest at seven weeks and will become independent shortly afterwards. If housed outdoors, the chipmunk will be less active in cold spells of weather.

SPINY MICE

Several different species of mouse are being bred by enthusiasts, of which the best known are probably spiny mice (*Acomys* species). Originating from parts of North Africa and the Middle East, these mice have unusual spiky fur, as their name suggests. Ideal housing for a spiny mouse would be a converted aquarium with a ventilated hood. Because of their small size, they may find a cage too spacious to make them feel secure. Care needs to be taken when handling these mice as their tails are easily injured. Damage to the tail can also result if the mice are housed in overcrowded accommodation, even if it is only for a relatively short time.

The breeding habits of spiny mice are unusual for small mammals. They have a long pregnancy, lasting around 38 days, and usually only give birth to two or three pups in one litter. The young are active almost from birth and are covered in grey fur at this stage. In addition to seeds and greenstuff, spiny mice will also eat mealworms.

SUGAR GLIDER

The small marsupial known as the sugar glider (*Petaurus breviceps*) originates from Australia and New Guinea. Its main diet should be a nectar solution mixed fresh each day. Fresh fruit and vegetables can also be provided, along with nuts and seeds, a few mealworms and other sources of protein, such as commercial dog or cat food.

Sugar gliders need indoor aviary-type housing, and it is a good idea to make sure this is easy to clean: the sticky nature of their droppings means that the gliders' quarters must be cleaned out on a daily basis.

A nest box for sleeping purposes should be included in their enclosure, and add tree branches, such as apple, to simulate their natural habitat and provide them with an opportunity for regular exercise.

As marsupials, the newborn young move after birth to their mother's pouch, where they will remain for the next ten weeks. Weaning occurs about five weeks later. Young sugar gliders mature at around ten months old and may go on to live for a decade or more.

+ ABOVE
A pair of sugar gliders. They require an aviary-like structure, equipped with branches to allow them to climb freely. Their quarters need to be designed so that they can be cleaned easily.

+ LEFT
Sugar gliders reproduce in a different way to the small mammals more usually kept as pets. They are marsupials, forming part of the group that includes kangaroos.

HEALTH CARE

Once established in their quarters, small animals usually prove to be very healthy. One of the more common causes of serious health problems in small mammals is a sudden change in their diet, which is likely to lead to digestive upsets. Treatment of these animals is not always straightforward because, in many cases, they will react adversely to certain antibiotics. Seeking veterinary advice early offers the best hope of recovery from illness.

SMALL MAMMAL HEALTH

◆ BELOW
Rabbits often need to have their claws trimmed back. If overgrown, walking will be difficult.

Once they are settled in their housing, small animals are usually healthy, and need very little in the way of routine health care. Sometimes though, you may need to clip back their claws if these become overgrown. If you prefer, you can ask your vet to do this for you. However, clipping claws is straightforward, provided that you have a suitable pair of clippers for the purpose.

Guillotine-type clippers with a sliding blade are to be recommended. This makes it easier to control the amount of the nail which you will be trimming off, as the claw is placed within the ring of the blade. It is helpful to have someone else to restrain your pet, so that you can concentrate on clipping the claw

safely. If left, the claws can otherwise curl back into the pad, causing great discomfort to the animal. Guinea pigs are most susceptible to overgrown claws, but rabbits can also suffer from this problem.

Carry out claw clipping in a good light, so that you can detect the quick, visible as a pink streak running down the claw from the base. You then need to cut at a point where this disappears towards the tip of the nail, so as to avoid bleeding. In the case of individuals with black claws, however, it may be impossible to spot the end of the quick, and particular care needs to be taken in these cases. If you do nick a claw too short, or it is injured and starts bleeding, pressing on the tip for a few moments should help to stem the blood flow. A styptic pencil, as sold in chemists (drug stores) for shaving nicks, may also help.

◆ BELOW LEFT
If the incisor teeth do not meet correctly in jaws, it will soon be impossible for the rabbit to continue eating.

◆ BELOW RIGHT
Hair loss is a relatively common condition in many of the smaller mammal breeds.

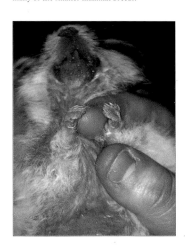

Overgrown teeth, caused by
malocclusion, when the top and
bottom incisors do not meet properly,
are a more serious proposition to deal
with, and these are best attended to
by your vet. The teeth are likely to
need trimming back every eight weeks
or so, to allow your pet to continue
eating without difficulty.

Nutritional problems are rare in
small animals, particularly now that
specially formulated diets are widely
available. Even so, cases of Vitamin C
deficiency do occur occasionally in
guinea pigs which, unlike other small
animals, cannot manufacture this
vital vitamin in their bodies. It must
therefore be present in their diet. If
you are housing a rabbit and guinea
pig together and offering them rabbit
pellets, then a deficiency, giving rise
to the condition known as scurvy, is
likely to occur before long. Dry,
flaky skin which can bleed readily
is the commonest sign. Vitamin C
supplements and regular use of a
guinea pig food, which will contain
this vitamin, should lead to a cure.

Hair thinning in hamsters is a sign
of old age rather than a nutritional
deficiency, and there is really nothing
that can be done about it. Equally,
another quite common condition
which is difficult to deal with in
elderly male guinea pigs is a distended
rectum, which leads to swelling as the
result of a build-up of faecal matter

here. This appears to be the result of
the loss of muscular tone. Increasing
the fibre content of the diet may help
but, ultimately, the rectum will need to
be emptied manually, gently massaging
the affected area with a little olive oil
first to loosen the obstruction. This
can be done at home but your vet can
perform it for you, if you prefer.

BACTERIAL ILLNESSES

♦ BELOW
Rabbits are prone to upper respiratory infections – a condition known as snuffles. A nasal discharge, as seen here, is one of the most common signs.

♦ BOTTOM
A sick guinea pig. A mite infestation which results in fur loss can lead to a more generalized illness if left untreated. This is the case for most small mammals.

It is not difficult to recognize signs of illness in a small animal as, when sick, an individual will usually be less active than normal and it may lose its appetite. It is likely to sit in a hunched-up fashion, with its fur held out from the body, creating a ruffled appearance. Even so, it can be very difficult to diagnose the cause of the illness accurately, because the symptoms of many infections are fairly similar.

As a result of their small size, pet rodents especially will lose heat rapidly from their bodies, which results in their condition deteriorating quickly. As a first step, therefore, it is important to provide some additional heat, while leaving a cooler area where your pet can retreat if it starts to feel too warm. A heat lamp will be useful for this purpose.

A small mammal that is sick needs urgent veterinary attention but, unfortunately, the choice of drugs which can be used to treat infections in this group of creatures is more restricted than in other pets because they react very badly to a number of antibiotics. Some antibiotics will have

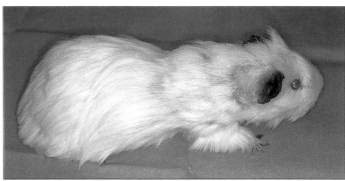

a harmful effect on the beneficial bacteria in the digestive tract, and this can prove fatal. You should never be tempted to use remedies prescribed for other pets for treatment purposes.

Young, recently-weaned rodents are perhaps most prone to bacterial illnesses, particularly if their diet is changed suddenly, because this can allow harmful bacteria to colonize the digestive tract, and interferes with the digestion of food. The stress of rehoming can also be significant.

Tyzzer's disease for example can strike young mice, rats and gerbils in particular. It is caused by a bacterium

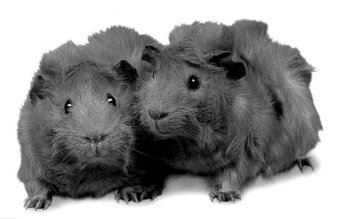

known as *Bacillus piliformis*, with symptoms typically including diarrhoea; sometimes in epidemics, a large number of young animals will die suddenly from this. Young hamsters can suffer from an infection known as wet tail, or proliferative ileitis, which again is often linked with a bacterial infection. Diarrhoea

♦ LEFT
Illnesses can be spread easily when guinea pigs are being housed together. This applies especially in the case of skin ailments, such as mites and ringworm.

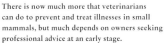

◆ BELOW
Health problems can be caused by unsuitable
bedding. Eye and associated nasal irritations
in gerbils can be triggered by allowing them
to burrow into fine sawdust.

◆ BELOW
There is now much more that veterinarians
can do to prevent and treat illnesses in small
mammals, but much depends on owners seeking
professional advice at an early stage.

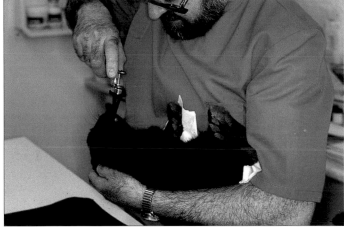

affecting the area under the tail causes the fur here to appear wet, while internally, the part of the small intestine known as the ileum will be badly inflamed. Again, treatment is difficult, but it can be successful, especially if carried out before the hamster becomes badly dehydrated.

Other illnesses may be more localized. Rats and mice are particularly vulnerable to infections of the upper respiratory tract, which result in runny noses and noisy breathing. Similar symptoms can be triggered by dust from unsuitable bedding, which will provoke an allergic reaction. Rapid treatment is vital before the infection spreads further down into the respiratory system, causing pneumonia. Rabbits can suffer from a similar condition, often referred to as snuffles.

Guinea pigs are especially prone to pneumonia, which can be caused by a range of different bacteria. This is often linked to poor ventilation in their quarters, or

damp surroundings, and there may be few, if any, early-warning symptoms. Only if the unfortunate guinea pig is autopsied will the cause of death become known. Laboured breathing

and loss of appetite are the most likely indicators of this problem. Antibiotic therapy may help a sick individual, although pneumonia in any small animal is a very serious condition.

◆ BELOW
You can prevent dental problems
in small mammals by providing
them with various chews, which
will help to keep their teeth in
good condition

VIRAL AND FUNGAL ILLNESSES

◆ BELOW
Myxomatosis is a killer viral disease which
relatively few rabbits will survive, and there
is no treatment available. All pet rabbits should
be protected by vaccination.

The most significant viral illnesses
for owners of small animals occur in
rabbits, and both have been developed
with a view to controlling wild rabbit
populations by biological means.

MYXOMATOSIS

This is a virus which can be spread
to domestic rabbits by wild rabbits
visiting their hutches; for this reason
it is recommended to stand hutches
at least 60 cm (2 ft) off the ground in
areas where wild rabbits are prevalent,
and to double-wire runs on both faces
of the timber around the perimeter.
Outbreaks of myxomatosis tend
to occur in the summer in more
temperate areas because biting insects,
such as mosquitoes, are also capable of
spreading the infection, and these are
most numerous at this time of year.

The earliest signs of infection are
inflammation of the eyes, quickly
accompanied by a whitish discharge.
By this stage, the rabbit will be
seriously ill and will have lost its
appetite. Sadly, there is no treatment
for myxomatosis, and most affected

individuals will die within a couple of
days. Those which survive beyond this
stage develop scabs around their eyes,
and their ears become badly swollen
and start to droop. With virtually no
hope of survival, therefore, it will be
kindest to have a rabbit which has
contracted myxomatosis painlessly

◆ BELOW LEFT
A guinea pig that is housed with a rabbit does
not need to be vaccinated against myxomatosis
or VHD, which only affect rabbits.

◆ BELOW
Ringworm on a rabbit's face. This fungal
ailment is usually characterized by its circular
pattern of spread, with accompanying hair loss.

♦ BELOW
A vaccine to protect against VHD being
administered. The vaccine is essential, especially
in exhibition stock, to guard against this
relatively common killer rabbit disease.

euthanased after diagnosis. In areas
where this infection crops up regularly,
it is vital to have pet rabbits protected
by vaccination, since they are more
vulnerable to the disease than wild
rabbits, which may have some
immunity to this illness. In areas
where a vaccine is not available, then,
keeping domestic rabbits isolated
from wild rabbits, and screening their
quarters from insects, should offer
some protection against myxomatosis.

VHD

Viral haemorrhagic disease (VHD) has
only been recognized in rabbits since
the 1980s, but has spread through the
wild population and infected domestic
stock as well. There are very few
symptoms, and an affected rabbit will
usually die suddenly. One tell-tale sign
is a slight haemorrhaging of blood
from the nose. There is no treatment,
and vaccination against this disease is
important, particularly for show stock
because the virus survives well in the
environment. It is spread by contaminated food and water bowls, housing
pens and even clothing, as well as
directly from one rabbit to another.

Because rabbits are prone to
digestive upsets, viruses may have a
role in some cases of digestive illness,
although the role is not yet clearly
understood. The hope of recovery
stems from preventing dehydration,
which accompanies severe diarrhoea,
from becoming life-threatening. This
should enable the body's own defence
mechanisms to overcome the illness.

RINGWORM

Viruses are less important to small
mammals such as hamsters, which are
usually housed on their own in the

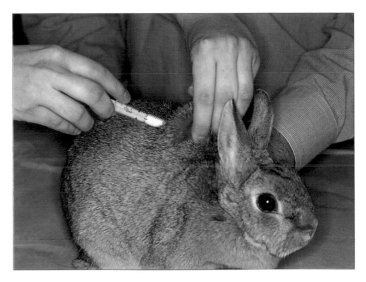

home, and are therefore at a much
reduced risk of acquiring this type of
infection. But, very occasionally, small
mammals may be afflicted by the
fungal disease called ringworm. This
causes a loss of the coat in circular
patches. The risk is that this condition
can be spread to human beings, where
it will show up as red blotches, in the
shape of circles, on the arm where the
infected area of fur was in contact with
the skin. Fortunately, it can be treated.

Ringworm is transmitted very
easily by fungal spores on grooming
equipment. If you suspect ringworm,
avoid using this on any other animal in
your collection. The spores will linger
in hutches and elsewhere for years,
so thorough disinfection is essential
after an outbreak, using a hexetidine
preparation to kill the fungus. Wear
gloves when cleaning out the quarters
and burn the bedding, which is likely
to be contaminated with spores.

♦ RIGHT
Hamsters rarely
suffer from viral
illnesses. However,
the hamster plague
virus will cause fits,
and an affected
hamster will die
within 24 hours.

PARASITIC ILLNESSES

Rabbits and guinea pigs in particular are both prone to external parasites living on their bodies. Rabbits can often suffer from ear mites, which cause the condition sometimes described as canker. The mites cause irritation within the ear canal, resulting in the formation of brown scabs here, with the resulting discomfort causing the rabbit to scratch its ears more frequently than normal. If left, the mites are likely to spread into the inner part of the ear, permanently damaging the rabbit's sense of balance.

Do not attempt to pick off the scabs but, instead, dust the ears with flower of sulphur, a yellow powder available from pharmacies, which will kill off the mites effectively. Disinfect the hutch thoroughly once the rabbit has recovered fully, to eliminate any risk of reinfection as far as possible, although there is a risk that the mites could be reintroduced on dusty bedding material such as hay.

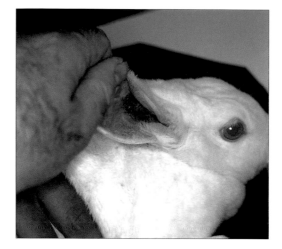

◆ LEFT
Ear mites attack the inside of the ear, creating brownish, crusty deposits here. These parasites can spread easily from rabbit to rabbit but can be treated easily.

Guinea pigs are vulnerable to skin mites, which again may lurk in contaminated bedding. You may miss the initial stages of infection, when the mites cause tiny white spots under the fur. Skin shedding, in the form of pronounced dandruff, then follows along with hair loss. At this stage, a

mite infestation may sometimes appear like ringworm, and skin scrapings from an affected area will be necessary to identify the mites under a microscope.

Treatment by injection, using the drug ivermectin at the appropriate dilution, is now the simplest way to kill off these mites, although this treatment will be needed over a period of a month or so, with injections being given every fortnight. The cage must also be thoroughly disinfected, to kill off any surviving mites. Other guinea pigs sharing the hutch will probably need to be treated as well. The susceptibility of guinea pigs to skin problems means that a thorough examination will be necessary to determine the cause of the problem, which is not always infectious. Some sows, for example, lose patches of their fur when pregnant, but this should regrow in due course.

It is always very important, particularly if your rabbit or guinea pig has suffered recently from diarrhoea,

◆ BELOW
Rex breeds of rabbit may suffer fur loss because of their housing conditions, rather than as a result of illness.

◆ BELOW
Diarrhoea in rats or mice can be caused by
parasites, but tests will need to be carried out
by your vet to obtain a definitive diagnosis.

◆ BELOW
A severe case of mange in a guinea pig.
Treatment by a series of injections will be
required, but always seek advice at an early
stage to minimize your pet's suffering.

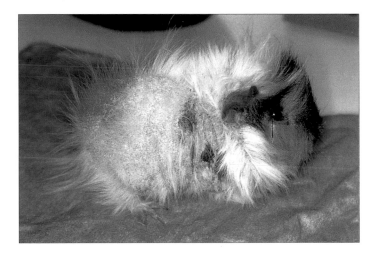

to check there is no soiling of the
fur around the animal's rear end.
Otherwise, your pet could become
parasitized by the larvae of blowflies,
responsible for the condition often
described as fly strike. Bluebottles
and similar flies will be attracted to
the soiled fur, laying their eggs here
which hatch rapidly into larvae.
These literally bore into the flesh,
releasing deadly toxins. This is why it
is so important to remove the larvae
without delay because, otherwise, they
will kill the rabbit or guinea pig. Your
vet will be able to remove them with
special forceps; a wound powder may
also be used to promote healing.

A wide range of microscopic, single-
celled organisms, called protozoa, can
be found in the intestinal tract of small
mammals, often helping to digest the
food here so that the nutrients can
be absorbed into the body. Some of
these protozoa are likely to be harmful,
however, giving rise to the disease
known as coccidiosis. They can cause
diarrhoea, which may be blood-stained,

and permanent damage to the lining
of the intestinal tract, so that a young
rabbit will not grow properly.

In order to protect against this
infection, drugs called coccidiostats
are sometimes incorporated in the
rabbit's food. Another form of the
infection attacks the liver, causing
what is described as hepatic
coccidiosis, which can also be fatal.

Actual treatment of coccidiosis will
be possible using specially formulated
sulphur-based compounds available
from your vet. Cleanliness is equally
vital, however, because the infection is
transmitted via the rabbit's droppings.

◆ BELOW
If you have a number of guinea pigs, use
separate grooming tools for them. This will
help to prevent the spread of skin mites.

Agouti a colour form of some mammals, including guinea pigs and rats; the agouti characteristic is shown by dark and light banding extending down the individiual hairs of the fur, creating a sparkling appearance.

Albino the abnormal lack of colour pigmentation in the hair, skin and eyes of animals and humans; albino animals will usually have white or colourless hair, pink skin and red or pink eyes.

Boar male guinea pig.

Breed domestic variant, usually a colour form, created by selective breeding.

Buck male rabbit.

Caecum large, blind-ending sac at the junction of the small and large intestines. Significant in rodents and rabbits; contains bacteria and protozoa essential for the digestive process.

Caviomorph a group of rodents; confined to the Americas. Includes guinea pigs and chinchillas.

Cavy alternative name for a guinea pig, derived from the generic name of *Cavia*.

Cubs name given to the young of certain species, including rats.

Doe female rabbit, mouse or rat.

Fancy selective breeding to display traits for exhibition purposes.

Gestation period the length of time that a female mammal carries her young prior to birth.

Incisors teeth at the front of the mouth.

Kittens name given to the young of some mammals, including cats and rabbits.

Kits young chinchillas.

Lagomorph collective name given to rabbits, hares and pikas.

Litter a number of animals born to the same mother at the same time.

Malocclusion failure of the teeth in the upper and lower jaws to meet correctly. A common problem in rodents and lagomorphs, which can lead to starvation.

Mammals group of vertebrates that suckle their young. Most give birth to live young, with very few laying eggs.

Marsupial group of mammals where the young are born in an immature state, and are reared in their mother's pouch where they can suckle.

Mastitis inflammation of the mammary glands seen in nursing mammals.

Metabolism the sum of all the chemical reactions occuring within the cells of any living organism, including mammals.

Mutation a change in the structure of a single gene, the arrangement of genes on a chromosome or the number of chromosomes in any living organism, including animals,

which may result in a change
in the appearance or behaviour
of the organism.

Myomorph major grouping
of rodents; includes rats, mice,
hamsters and gerbils.

Outcrossing pairing to avoid
inbreeding between a male and
female.

Protozoa microscopic single-
celled organisms; can be beneficial
as aids to food digestion in
herbivores, or can cause various
diseases.

Rex mutation resulting in a curly
rather than straight coat; seen in
various small mammals, including
guinea pigs.

Ringworm fungal disease seen
in small animals; can be spread
to human beings.

Rodents biggest group of
mammalian species; distinguished
by their dentition pattern,
particularly the sharp incisor
teeth at the front of the jaws.

Scurvy the effect of Vitamin C
deficiency, resulting in skin
problems.

Show standard description of the
ideal example of a breed, used for
judging purposes; specifies not just
the physical appearance but also
other features, such as coloration,
for which points are awarded.
Also referred to as the standard.

Sow female guinea pig.

Tortoiseshell a colour form of
some mammals, including guinea
pigs, hamsters and cats. The fur
has yellow, brown or black
markings, which can also be
combined with white.

Type description of a creature's
physical appearance; used in show
circles, especially for small mammals.

Weaning the process by which
a young mammal is accustomed
to take food other than its
mother's milk.

Further Reading

Although some of the books listed below may be out of print, they can often be obtained without difficulty through public libraries or from secondhand bookstores specializing in petcare.

Alderton, David (1986)
A Petkeeper's Guide to Rabbits & Guinea Pigs
Salamander Books/Interpet

Alderton, David (1986)
A Petkeeper's Guide to Hamsters & Gerbils
Salamander Books/Interpet

Alderton, David (1997)
The International Encyclopedia of Pet Care
Howell Book House

Bielfield, Horst (1985)
Mice: A Complete Pet Owners Manual
Barron's Educational Series Inc.

Edsel, Graham J. (1997)
Guide to Owning a Guinea Pig: Housing, Feeding, Breeding, Exhibition, Health Care

Gendron, Karen, and Earle Bridges, Michele (2000)
The Rabbit Handbook (Barron's Pet Handbooks)
Barron's Educational Series Inc.

Gurney, Peter (1997)
Piggy Potions
Kingdom Books

Gurney, Peter (1999)
Proper Care of Guinea Pigs
Kingdom Books

Henwood, Chris (1985)
Rodents in Captivity
Ian Henry Publications

James, Carolina (1997)
The Really Useful Bunny Guide
T. F. H./Kingdom

Kotter, Engelbert (1999)
Gerbils
Barron's Educational Series Inc.

McKay, Jimmy (1991)
The New Hamster Handbook
Blandford Press

Mays, Nick (1993)
The Proper Care of Fancy Rats
T. F. H. Publications

Roder-Thiede, Maike (1999)
Chinchillas – A Complete Pet Owner's Manual
Barron's Educational Series Inc.

Sandford, J. C. (1996)
The Domestic Rabbit
Blackwell Science

Somerville, Barbara, and Buscis, Gerry (2000)
Training Your Pet Rat
Barron's Educational Series Inc.

Taylor, David (1996)
Small Pet Handbook
HarperCollins

Vanderlip, Sharon L. (1999)
Dwarf Hamsters: Everything About Purchase, Care, Feeding, and Housing (Barron's Complete Pet Owner's Manual)
Barron's Educational Series Inc.

Verhoef-Verhallen, Esther (1998)
Encyclopedia of Rabbits and Rodents
Rebo Productions

Suppliers

UNITED KINGDOM

Grange Aviaries & Pet Centre
Woodhouse Lane
Southampton SO30 2EZ
Tel: (01489) 781260

The Hutch Company
Parham Road
Kent CT1 1DD
Tel: (01227) 470470

Pet Essentials Ltd
1 Boundary Road
Hove
East Sussex BN3 4EH
Tel: (01273) 381517

Safari Select
Warren Farm
Sundridge
Kent TN14 6EE
Tel: (01959) 562193

Squashes
Robin Hood Mill, Lever Street
Bolton
Lancashire BL3 6NE
Tel: (01204) 535 357

UNITED STATES

Earthwise Animal Catalog
P. O. Box, 654 Millwood
NY 10546
Tel: (212) 787-6100

Natural Animal
7000 US 1 North
St Augustine, FL 32095
Tel: (1-800) 274-7387

Nature Pet Care Company
8050 Lake City Way
Seattle, WA 98115
Tel: (1-800) 962-8266

Pet Guard
165 Industrial Loop South
Orange Park, FL 32073
Tel: (1-800) 874-3221

Real Goods Trading Company
966 Mazzoni Street
Ukiah, CA 95482-3471
Tel: (1-800) 762-7325

Whole Animal Resource Store
911 Cedar Street
Santa Cruz, CA 95060
Tel: (408) 458-3475

www.bunny-rabbits-guinea-pigs-pet-mice-and-more.com
www.pet-parade.com
www.drsfostewrsmith.com

CANADA

Pets West
Broadmead Village Shopping Center
Royal Oak Drive
Victoria
Tel: (250) 744-1779

Paws 'N' Jaws
N. Gate Shopping Mall
Regina
SK 99833
Tel: (306) 545 7387

AUSTRALIA

Oxford Pet Supplies
350 Oxford Street
Bondi Junction
NSW 2022
Tel: (02) 9389 9294

Pet City
224 Wishart Road
Mt Gravatt
QLD 4122
Tel: (04) 3319 2086

Pets Paradise
Shop 35, Gilchrist Drive
Campbelltown
NSW 2560
Tel: (02) 46325 2855

NEW ZEALAND

Pet Planet
Whangaparaoa Shopping Centre
  (Upper Pacific Plaza)
P.O. Box 268
Whangaparaoa
Tel: (09) 424 4353

ACKNOWLEDGEMENTS

The author, photographer and publishers would like to thank the following for their help and co-operation in making this book:

Ian Abercrombie, J. Ansley, S. & R. Badger, S. Bagley, Harriet Bartholomew & Flora, Jonathan Bartholomew, Stephen Bartholomew, P. Beaven, G. Black, S. L. Bond, S. Bradley, Jane Burton, J. & P. Canning, William Church, Ian Cinderby, M. Clark, Peter Curry, P. J. Daniels, Carley Deanus, Dawn Deanus, Lauren Deanus, Vanessa Dyer, Jill Fagg, Sue Fisher, Emma Freeman, V. A. Harris, Alison Hay, James Hay, Wade & Kirby Heames, H. Hewitt, Debra Hodson, B. Hollandt, J. & D. Johnson, Duane Joy, A. E. Kensit, Simon Gardner, L. Graham, Jo King, Graham Knott, Simon Langdale, Jenny Lavender, Rosie Lowen, Jeanette Marina, M. J. McLellan, M. Peacock, L. & A. Piatnauer, B. & L. Riddy, Mary Rodriguez, Jackie Roswell, Steve Rudd, Britta Stent, Kevin Stevens, Wendy Stevens, Antonia Swierzy, N. P. Tabony, Anne Terry, B. Terry, J. Ward, Angela Warrell, A. Wells, Cathy Whitehead, Charlotte Whitehead.

PICTURE CREDITS

t=top; b=bottom; c=centre; l=left; r=right

BBC Natural History Unit:
Niall Benvie 2, 8t; **Jim Clare** 72b; **Hanne and Jens Eriksen** 88b; **Jürgen Freund** 44c; **Andrew Harrington** 9t; **Steven David Miller** 81t, 81b; **Chris O'Reilly** 8b; Pete Oxford 72t, 73b; **Andrey Zvoznikov** 26br.
Bruce Coleman Collection:
Erwin and Peggy Bauer 52t; **Jane Burton** 6, 26t, 38b, 39t, 70t, 71b, 74b, 75tl; **Werner Layer** 74t; **Robert Maier** 43t, 53tr, 75tr; **Hans Reinhard** 62t, 62b, 71tl; **Kim Taylor** 42b, 63t; **Jörg and Petra Wegner** 29t, 30t, 30c, 30b, 31t, 31c, 31b, 40t, 43b, 71tl, 84b; **Günter Ziesler** 26bl.
W. G. V. Lewis MRCVS 82br, 83tr.
Dermod Malley FRCVS 82t, 82bl, 83tl, 83b, 84t, 84c, 85t, 86t, 86br, 87t, 88t, 89.
Warren Photographic:
Jane Burton 7, 38tl, 38tr, 52b, 53tl, 53b, 56c, 56bl, 61tl, 61tr, 61cl, 61br, 75br, 79tc, 79tr, 79c, 79bl, 79br, 85b.

INDEX